How to Turn Words into Money

How to Turn Words into Money

Leverage These Proven Magic Words Into Millions

Ted Nicholas

Nicholas Direct Inc.

© Copyright 2004 by Ted Nicholas
Nicholas Direct, Inc.
P.O. Box 877
Indian Rocks Beach, FL 33785
website: http://www.tednicholas.com

Printed in the United States of America
First Printing January 2004
ISBN 1-887741-01-1

Contents

A Word From The Author   1

Introduction   3

Words, Not Numbers, Are the True Currency of Business   5

How to Pay Less For Everything   7

The Education of a Salesman   10

The Future of Direct Marketing   23

How To Generate Great Ideas   36

How Many of These 17 Commonly Accepted Myths Are Blocking Your Path to Real Success?   48

How To Make Your Company An Everlasting Success   60

How To Create a Successful U.S.P.   70

How To Create a Spiritual Company and Turn It Into a Multi-Million Dollar Success   80

How To Generate Energy—The Fuel of Success   91

10 Million Dollar Sales Secrets   104

How To Prepare Headlines That Make Money   117

Secrets of a Profitable Ad   126

33 Secrets of Successful Sales Letters   137

Secrets of Envelope 'Teaser' Copy Which Can *Double* Your Response — 149

38 Ways to Use FREE—the Most Powerful Word In Any Language — 160

How To Launch a Hot New Product — 172

How To Prepare a Successful Mailing Kit That Transcends Language Barriers — 187

How To Profit From Public Speaking — 205

Secrets of Writing a Book That Sells — 220

So You Want To Do An Infomercial — 232

Secrets of Profitable Yellow Page Advertising — 242

How to Increase Wealth By Licensing Your Product Overseas! — 252

How To Use Two-Step Marketing to Return a Profit of $29,450 For Every 1,000 Leads! — 261

Is Money Important or Not? — 269

How Ted Nicholas Can Help You Further — 281

Share Your Success Story — 282

A Word From The Author

Words are more powerful than any army.

Swifter than a light beam.

Words can ruin friendships.

Cause pain, conflict and even war.

Words can increase love, life's most powerful emotion.

And sow a calm serenity in life.

Words can attract people to you, or drive them away.

Words can persuade others to take all sorts of actions. Go to war. Or march for peace. To laugh. To cry. Or to buy.

Words in your "self-talk" can make you sad or happy.

Choose words you say to yourself or to others with the utmost care.

Introduction

I love all forms of art. And, while of course I'm biased, I believe the written word is the most powerful form. Why? Words can create magic in your life. Certain words can make you rich. Successful. Happy. Enthusiastic. Content. Proud. That's why I coined the phrase "Magic Words."

Here is an example of the power of words. To be invited to one special seminar that I conduct, you must already be a millionaire.

I've noted that attendees to this "Millionaire Only" event have varying business backgrounds and history. I've had book authors, speakers, business owners, songwriters and executives. All are entrepreneurs.

But all these millionaire attendees have one thing in common. Each one could be placed in any city in the world flat broke, without contacts or even knowing the language. Within one year they would again be millionaires.

What is their one common characteristic? The ability to choose the words which make a sales message successful.

That's the underlying reason I wrote this book. I believe the best way I can help you is to help you craft successful sales messages.

Of course, the "vehicles" you use to deliver your sales messages will vary. You may use or plan to use one or several of the following.

Internet. Public speaking. Radio. T.V. Space ads. Direct mail. Card decks.

Perhaps your message may be contained in a song or jingle.

What qualifies me to author this topic? I probably earn more money *per word* than anyone living today. This includes books, speeches, tapes and advertising copy.

I've earned as much as $1,000,000 from a single full-page ad. From a seminar given just once. I've also earned seven figures on tape sets. I'll reveal how you can do the same.

This book is devoted to millionaires in three categories:

1. Prospective
2. Present
3. Former

Words, Not Numbers, are the True Currency of Business

Why are words so very important?

First, we think in words. Plus, the words we use in our "self-talk" are solely responsible for our emotions.

Both physical and mental food promote either good or poor health.

Clearly, physical food can nourish or harm our body depending on our choices. But here is an indisputable fact seldom mentioned by anyone.

You are the author of all your feelings

Negative mental food also has disastrous consequences. Use negative self talk, as do most people, and you will be poor as a result. Depression, failure, illness and even an early death are other strong possibilities.

Alternatively, choosing certain positive words in your self-talk will inevitably result in success, happiness and wealth. Plus, it increases the odds you will attain robust health.

Money is not the only form of wealth

While the main thrust of this journey you are about to take is financial success, you will also enrich yourself in ways that may be far more important to you than money alone.

As previously discussed, words trigger feelings. Our emotions are primarily responsible for the quality of our lives. What would life be without passion? Enthusiasm? Love? Inspiration?

I will reveal emotional words and phrases that invoke strong feelings. In others. And within yourself.

Master them and the result will be greater personal and business success. And greater financial wealth if you so desire.

Plus, you may become a more emotional, happy, compassionate and attractive person that others will gravitate toward.

So, let's start now. Join with me on this reading adventure.

I promise you I will do all I can to help you sing the song you came to sing!

How to Pay Less for Everything

"A penny saved is a penny earned," states the wise old saying which is so full of wisdom.

Imagine how much it would be worth to you if the rest of your life you got a big discount on future purchases, a favorable result of a personal question or request. You'll have a lot of fun, as I do, getting discounts up to 80% of the "normal" price.

I have developed "Magic Phrases" that come close to 100% success when you go to buy anything!

Best of all, there is no downside risk. In those rare situations when you do not achieve a better price, nothing bad happens. You are in no worse a position than when you started.

And, remember this.

When you don't ask, the answer is always NO!

Here are the most effective "Magic Phrases":

1. What is your very best price?
2. Is this your very best price?
3. Is this price negotiable?
4. Can you please do better than this price?

5. What is your best business rate?
6. Can you give me your lowest future sales discount now?
7. Can I have a 20% discount if I buy two?
8. Can you please extend me the same price as your best customer?
9. I always buy at a discount. Can you give me your best near wholesale price?
10. I'd like to reserve the most romantic table in your restaurant tonight for a special occasion. Can you please arrange to do this?

To increase your chance of success, these magic words and phrases must be used verbatim.

Practice them out loud in front of a mirror. Your body language is also very important. Say the "Magic Phrases" with a smile, making eye contact. Make sure the tone of your voice is strong and confident.

Below is a list of products and services where you can use the "Magic Phrases." Next to them are numbers of the "Magic Phrases" that may be applicable.

Hotel room 2, 5	Magazine advertisement 1, 2, 3, 4, 7
Jewelry 1, 2, 8, 10	Radio commercial 1, 2, 3, 4, 7
Clothing 6, 7, 8	Printing 1, 2, 3, 5
Shoes 6, 7, 8	Photography 1, 2, 3, 5
Antiques 3, 12	Banquet 1, 2, 3, 5
Car rental 1, 5	Legal services 1, 2, 3, 4
Wedding reception 1, 2, 4	Restaurant reservation 1, 2, 3, 4

It's fun to go through life buying everything you want at a significant discount. Use these "Magic Phrases" with care. When the people with whom you come in contact recognize that while you love discounts you treat everyone with dignity and respect, better prices will accrue to you on a daily basis.

Tips: *As with every word you ever state, body language as well as pauses, are very important.*

- Make eye contact
- Smile
- Speak clearly
- Nod your head slowly in a yes motion as you speak
- When you ask a question, pause and wait for a response. Resist the tendency to speak before the person you are with has the chance to answer

Practice the "Magic Phrases" and body language in front of a mirror. You'll get better and more effective as time goes on.

The Education of a Salesman

Being an effective salesman is a key reason for being able to live the kind of life I currently enjoy.

I assist clients from several continents in marketing their products and services.

Today, while traveling throughout the world, I continue to create copy which builds sales. It is truly a dream life.

My sales and marketing track record is what causes people to seek me out. The reason is simple—everyone needs more sales.

However, throughout my career I've observed that the sales process is completely misunderstood by most people. Selling is often considered a necessary evil. Many believe that advertising must be untruthful in order to successfully sell products. The Hollywood stereotype doesn't help either. For example, the tragic character of Willy Loman in Arthur Miller's play "Death of a Salesman" is often assumed to be typical.

As I see it, sales is a necessary profession in any free society. It's one of the most noble professions. Indeed, no free market system is possible unless goods and services are effectively sold.

Moreover, people in all fields benefit from improving their sales skills. Not just those who are directly connected with sales. Why?

Ideas must be sold!

Regardless of your job, profession, or business, it's not possible to function in the real world unless others accept your ideas. Of course, this is also fundamental to the sale of a product.

Among *Webster's* definitions of selling is this: "to establish faith, confidence, or belief in; to persuade (someone) of the value of something; convince."

It's easy to see how professional communicators, teachers, authors and public speakers need to sell their ideas to be effective.

But what about other fields that are not usually associated with sales? How about an architect, lawyer, doctor or Army officer? Do these people also need sales skills?

The answer is a resounding **"yes!"** It's been my experience and observation that those at the top in the above fields, along with their specialized expertise, are also outstanding sales people.

As to entrepreneurs and executives, clearly there is a direct relationship between their level of success and their ability to sell.

In the business world, to lead, inspire and motivate employees, raise capital, or negotiate with suppliers, considerable sales skills are required.

I've recently given a lot of thought to the life experiences that have influenced my views regarding the role of sales.

I thought a brief history and lessons derived therefrom might be helpful to your evolution as a marketer.

Early role models—my parents

My parents owned a successful restaurant. There were two keys to their success. My father oversaw the preparation of good food. But my mother, who was the hostess, was perhaps even more important. She was a terrific sales person. She had the ability to make everyone who came in for a meal feel welcome. Customers would seek her out as they returned again and again.

How did Mother win people over? Smiling warmly and making eye contact, she greeted everyone by name. She initiated conversation by asking questions about friends, family, vacations, etc. Upon seating them she developed a simple but effective technique. She immediately passed out menus without the usual delay waiting for the waiter or waitress to do so. Plus, she always asked this question: "What would you like to drink?" Even if there is a delay, people are happy in a restaurant if they promptly have a drink in their hands while they wait.

Think about how rarely you experience such treatment during your restaurant visits. My mother's rapport-building ability was at least as responsible for a waiting line of restaurant customers as the food that was served.

Teachers and coaches

A few teachers in school also taught me valuable sales lessons. The most fascinating subjects were so incredibly boring when an unenthusiastic instructor droned in a monotone about them. Yet, an enthusiastic teacher made all the difference. I found I got excited about even the most mundane subject with an instructor who was a good communicator.

I'll never forget Mrs. Price, my third grade teacher. I'm forever indebted to her for making American history so meaningful to me. She really "sold" me on the importance of the heroic deeds of our founding fathers.

My coaches in different sports also taught me a lot about the power of communication. For example, when Mr. Coleman, my high school basketball coach, delivered inspiring pre-game and half-time presentations, we got so fired up I and my team members felt we could beat the world! And we nearly did, becoming conference champions.

Relatives

My Uncle Frank was my favorite relative and a role model for me. He was a successful businessman. He owned four thriving restaurants and a lot of real estate. And he was a great salesman! He convinced investors to back him. He motivated employees and charmed customers better than anyone I had ever seen before.

Uncle Frank also showed me that one could live a balanced life, not be a workaholic, and still be successful. He balanced playing golf, traveling, spending time with his children and me, and social activities with business activities. I've done my best to emulate Uncle Frank all my life.

Books which had a great impact

Ever notice that people and books are the two sources from which we learn the most? People I found in books influenced me a great deal. I began pursuing a lifelong interest—reading biographies. Many inspired me to become more like them. A few people who made a huge difference to me include:

- Winston Churchill
- Henry Ford
- Frank W. Woolworth
- Booker T. Washington
- Bernard Gimbel
- Milton Hershey
- Aristotle
- Leonardo da Vinci
- Columbus
- Andrew Carnegie

The author having the most impact on me was the late Ayn Rand. Her books *The Fountainhead*, *We The Living*, *Anthem*, and *Atlas Shrugged* communicated convincingly perhaps the hardest thing of all to sell—a rational philosophy called objectivism.

Speakers who could sell their message

During my late teens and early 20's I began going to hear well-known speakers and lecturers make presentations. I also listened to their recordings. I was struck by what terrific sales people they were. Napoleon Hill was 84 years old when I saw him speak so effectively. Zig Ziglar was delivering almost the same powerful message then as he does now. Earl Nightingale's recording "Lead the Field" was masterfully presented. J. Douglas Edwards' speech "Closing the Sale" was very moving as well.

Two of the greatest communicators ever in my opinion are Billy Graham and Robert Schuller. These ministers deliver a message so powerful large numbers of people are persuaded to change their lives.

A forerunner to my sales training

My sales education has been a lifelong process which is never ending. However, much of what I discovered had nothing whatsoever to do with actually selling a product. For example, my dating experience was very important. Here's why.

My friends and I were interested in dating, especially in high school. And, naturally, the most attractive, intelligent, and/or personable females were the most appealing to us. But my friends rarely would ask them out. Why? They dreaded the feeling of rejection if the answer was "no!" Plus, most of them didn't really feel worthy of the girls in whom they were most interested.

To me, this was truly an amazing phenomenon. The prettiest, smartest girls with great personalities were rarely asked out on dates. They were actually asked out less than others precisely because they were special and appealing. Even by the most intelligent, attractive boys.

In thinking about this, I decided that I was worthy of any classmate's company. I simply felt I had a lot to offer.

I also figured if I invited someone out, the worst that could happen didn't seem so bad. A prospective date could say "no." So I began experimenting.

I was pleasantly surprised. The first few times I asked the most appealing girl I could think of out on a date she said "yes!"

I'm sure this had far less to do with how attractive I may have been or how I presented myself. It really was something far different. Here is the real key.

The willingness to risk getting a "no"!

I discovered a valuable truth which made all the difference. Throughout my life it's not changed. Few people are willing to put themselves on the line for anything. Be it a date. The chance of a rewarding personal relationship. The pursuit of a business loan. Or asking for an order.

During this important time of self-discovery, I identified two other key points.

1. *Getting a "no" doesn't have to feel like a rejection.* And even if it does hurt a little until you retrain yourself, the feeling won't last long. It also won't kill you or do any permanent damage.

2. *You can actively control every feeling you ever have.* Our emotions do not depend on what happens to us. The *meaning*

you give all events and experiences in life determines the emotion you experience.

So, I began mentally preparing myself for any rejection I might encounter in dating through the use of "self-talk." I reminded myself of the worthwhile qualities I had to offer any prospective girlfriend. If these were not seen or acknowledged, I convinced myself that was her problem, not mine!

Interestingly, the first time I was turned down for a date actually didn't feel bad at all. Here is what happened. I called Carol L. and asked her to go to a school dance. She said while she appreciated my asking, she couldn't accept the invitation. She had a boyfriend from out of town who was taking her to the dance.

While I was disappointed, she was very nice about how she handled the call. In reality, I was glad to know how things stood with her. Plus, I opened the door to the future by letting her know I was interested. In fact, the next year Carol told me she wasn't seeing her former boyfriend any longer. Thereafter, we went out together several times and became good friends.

My male friends' actions continued to surprise me. They told me they would still feel personally rejected, even if a girl they approached turned them down for no other reason than having an out-of-town boyfriend they didn't know about! So they stayed home and pined away.

The secret of being successful at having a rewarding dating experience is simple. You may be turned down occasionally. Or even often. You may even feel rejected at times. But each time you get a "no" the odds shift in your favor. Best of all, going ahead and facing your fears, and asking out attractive people practically assures you of a fabulous social life! I'm sure you can see how this relates to my sales education.

Door-to-door sales taught me a lot

After just a semester of college at Susquehanna University, I dropped out for two reasons. I didn't feel I was learning much about starting my own business and my goal of becoming an entrepreneur. Plus, I wanted to assist my father, who had become ill, in the family restaurant business.

I helped my father run his seasonal restaurant, open only during the summer. In the fall I looked for something to do during the winter. Answering a classified ad, I took a commission-only job selling Kirby vacuum cleaners.

And my life changed forever.

While making sales calls I discovered an amazing truth. On a cold call it was possible to sell expensive, high-quality products to homeowners.

I was really lucky to learn about door-to-door sales. I also had the good fortune of experiencing Kirby's terrific training program conducted by a great sales manager.

What I learned about professional sales absolutely fascinated me. It still does! Imagine. It's possible to meet a complete stranger at their home and sell them a vacuum cleaner for over $1,000 just an hour or so later! It seemed like a miracle.

I produced more sales than anyone in the office. Why? A big key was I knocked on more doors than my colleagues. I got more noes than anyone else. But I also got more people to say "yes!" The real payoff was increased self-confidence. I figured if I could sell direct to homeowners on cold calls, I could do anything!

However, my lifelong dream was one day to have my own company. I felt if I went into a business for myself and it flopped, I really had nothing to fear. I now had a psychological escape hatch. For I could always return to door-to-door selling anytime I wished and make big money.

The biggest lesson gained from successfully selling vacuum cleaners was this. In sales, as in dating, the key is in what I call the "next" technique. As and when you are turned down, you simply thank the person for their time and attention. Then you say to yourself—**"next"**

The real secret. You immediately go on to the *next* prospect!

But what do most people do? After a rejection or two. Or 10. Or 100. Or 1,000. They quit!

In sales, after a few doors are slammed in your face or when people don't buy your product, it can be tempting to completely give up.

But, as with dating, I discovered when you are turned down, nothing bad happens! You don't die. Or become ill. You simply say "next."

As anyone who has done it knows, selling one-on-one is not easy. Direct sales has been defined as "the highest paid hard job and the lowest paid easy job in the world." The reason?

The reality is most prospects say "no," then "yes" to any offer. But few people have enough self-esteem to handle what can feel like constant rejection. However, the ones who do are very successful. And very rich!

There is an effective way to sell that can generate huge worldwide sales and profits easily and *without* personal rejection. Of course, I'm referring to *direct marketing*.

Here is what led me to marketing direct to consumers. Instead of live selling I now use letters, ads, card decks, TV, radio and the Internet in lieu of a sales force!

Direct marketing— the easiest way to sell anything!

My first business was Peterson's House of Fudge, a candy and ice cream shop. Products were made before the public in an open kitchen. From the beginning I used billboards as a unique form of direct marketing.

Promotions for the business at first consisted of a series of roadside signs beginning 20 miles away from the shop. Each of the signs had a different message, such as:

"See candy made"

"Free samples"

"77 flavors of fudge"

"Hand-dipped chocolates"

When I changed copy on the signs, more or less people stopped to shop. Thus, I could see the *power of the words* in action. Some words worked better than others in getting people to stop at my store. This was invaluable knowledge.

I confirmed the truth first discovered by John Kennedy in 1920: "Advertising copy is salesmanship in print."

By the time I was 29 I had 30 retail shops in six states in operation. I prepared a catalog which offered all my products and was given to each store customer. Plus, I sent a copy to my mailing list. As I improved copy, results got better and better. Sales continued to grow and . . . **I was hooked!**

Sales generated by catalog both delighted and amazed me.

The fact I could do a big business by mail seemed like magic! Plus, I could use sales techniques learned from selling vacuum cleaners, add my growing knowledge of the power of the printed word, and new customers who had never, ever been to my shops ordered my products. Not only that. They enclosed money in advance of my company shipping the product! No collection problems.

When I realized the implications, I really got excited! Now I could sell my products not just in my shops, but worldwide. And as I began mailing my catalog to my growing list of customers, sales increased dramatically.

A new career as an author and publisher

A few years later I wrote my first book, HOW TO FORM YOUR OWN CORPORATION WITHOUT A LAWYER FOR UNDER $75. But nine publishers turned it down. They didn't think it would sell. I thought they were wrong, so I decided to publish and direct market the book myself.

I formed a new company, Enterprise Publishing. And ran my first advertising—a $90 classified ad in the *Wall Street Journal*. This ad attracted a few hundred inquiries. I followed up the leads with mailing a brochure and sales letter. I got back close to $400 in orders! I went on from there to larger and larger ads in numerous magazines and newspapers as well as direct mail.

Within six months I ran my first full-page ad, which was a huge success.

Advertising success led to a profitable publishing company and numerous other ventures. One very successful business I founded is The Company Corporation, which provides low-cost incorporating services. This company, which I sold in 1991 along with the publishing business, is the largest company of its kind in the world with over 200,000 clients!

My growing sales skills combined with the power of direct marketing fueled the success of my companies. Best of all, you can always learn more. I discover exciting new things about sales and marketing every day. I love being in a field where there is no end or limit to your skills! What about you?

10 sales lessons anyone can put to use

1. Direct marketing to consumers is the *most effective way to sell anything to anyone*.

2. You can sell products and services *worldwide without a sales force* or *employees*.

3. *Words* used in sales copy make a *dramatic difference in response*.

4. Direct marketing is the *cheapest* way to sell. (For example, the total cost of an average personal sales call today is approximately $550.

5. Since you don't meet prospects personally, you *never have to suffer personal rejection*.

6. Direct marketing is the *most scientific* selling method known. You can test every aspect in a small way before larger investments are made.

7. Direct marketing is the *only measurable* selling method as every ad, sales letter, card deck, TV or radio commercial, and Internet website can be coded, so you know the exact profit or loss on each of them.

8. Direct marketing knowledge is rare. Very *few people* (probably less than 100) in the entire world have the know-how to direct market properly.

9. You can operate *anywhere*. Direct marketing *opportunities abound* in the U.S. as well as in other developed and emerging countries.

10. Proven *techniques* that *work in personal sales* can be incorporated in direct marketing.

If you want to succeed in a big way, study all elements of the selling process. Ideally, take a job in direct sales as part of your training. As a serious student of direct marketing, you have an unparalleled opportunity to create a worldwide business. From experience, I know your future success is limited only by your imagination.

I look forward to hearing about your successes as well as your setbacks, both great teachers. You can be sure I'll report on mine.

The Future of Direct Marketing

I'm going to take a hard look at what every thinking person I know wonders about—the future of direct marketing.

There are three sections in this chapter:

    I. Predictions

   II. Direct Marketing principles that will not change

  III. Actions that best capitalize on future direct marketing opportunities

Predictions

As I gaze into my crystal ball, here is what I see happening in the next 5 to 10 years. I predict we're entering the realm of:

1. Customized products

The heyday of many mass produced products may soon be over. One size fits all will be replaced with *one size fits one*!

Here are some examples. *Information products*, including books, audio and video tapes, and C.D.'s, can be designed to suit the wants, interests and needs of customers. You are asked some key questions. Then your book or tape can be individually tailored and produced for you.

Computers, for example, are already being built to order according to an individual's needs and wants. Leading companies like Dell Computer, now a multi-billion dollar company, are currently doing "mass customization." Formerly technology driven, Dell is now marketing driven. They operate with virtually no inventory.

More software will be made to order.

Automobiles will soon be custom built according to your individual needs, with a driver's seat made for your size, weight and body shape.

Services will be individually customized. For example, right now instead of a group class my wife, Bethany, now has an individually tailored exercise program at La Prairie in Clarens, Switzerland, a cutting-edge fitness center. Exercise equipment now exists that automatically programs for height, weight, strength, and age.

2. Worldwide marketing opportunities will grow . . .

. . . even for tiny virtual corporations. It's easier and easier to do business around the world via direct sales and licensing. Through licensees, we're now selling Nicholas Direct products in 123 countries.

The Internet now allows you to run a business from anywhere in the world. Many firms will set up virtual businesses in favorable offshore jurisdictions.

I have traveled for months doing seminars, etc. throughout Australia, New Zealand, Hong Kong, Mexico, Canada and the Caribbean. I communicated daily with my office, clients and family. I wrote copy, worked on a new book and ran several businesses, all via the Internet and faxes!

While I'm personally a beneficiary of the new innovations, I don't spend hours playing with the Internet. I prefer spending my time marketing products and concepts. Those who know me well are aware that I don't write copy on a computer either. Therefore, I'm lucky to have Bethany accompany me on trips. She's the family technical wizard! That's why I call her my "secret weapon." Plus, I engage some of the world's best people as independent contractors to help us on technical issues.

3. *Interactive marketing*—Two-way capability on virtually every medium

You will be talking to customers, answering questions, etc., on TV and via the computer.

Excellent customer service will cease to be just a slogan which everyone agrees on in theory but even today few practice. Incredibly, most web based as well as direct marketing companies I've seen have ineffective customer service policies and poorly trained people. No company will be able to survive in the next few years without highly responsive, well-trained customer service people.

4. Convergence of Internet, television, telephone and fax

It will soon be possible to have just one piece of equipment integrating all technical capabilities.

5. High digital TV (HDTV)

HDTV is an enhancement that will be tied to the Internet. This will allow instant ordering of products, interactive games, on-demand movies and other services.

Soon TV will be as sophisticated as the computer and "Internet ready" with two-way voice and fax communications.

6. Lower cost communications

Programs exist now to use the Internet to speak with other Internet users without paying long distance charges.

Continued improvements have resulted in faster speed of Internet connections.

7. Segmentation of potential customers

There will continue to be more small "niche" audiences available to whom you can direct highly targeted offers. Also, more offers will be personalized.

8. Loss of power by major TV networks

There will be an increased number of cable and satellite TV stations numbering in the hundreds, possibly the thousands.

We're finding currently some of our best direct marketing results on our TV infomercial occur not on big network stations, but on tiny independent cable and satellite stations.

9. Internet will probably become more entertainment driven

More sophisticated games, movies, "how to" information educational programs and other video products will be downloaded to your TV in seconds.

10. Customized news

Due to "information overload," better news filtering software programs will appear. Already existing are programs that will build a custom daily newspaper just for you based on your areas of interest. Soon this will be improved to include video and audio services.

11. Business on the Internet

In addition to news and entertainment, the Internet will be used more and more to handle business transactions.

Our Internet business from virtually no sales in early 1995 continues to grow on the Internet. A big reason is the change in the type of individual signing on, who is more receptive to buying opportunities.

12. Financial privacy—Technology will counter the effects of big government

Encryption will allows for more privacy in financial transactions on the Internet. Governments are already concerned as they fear loss of tax revenues from "invisible transactions."

Already several banks allow you to conduct transactions in complete privacy. You can transfer funds, exchange currencies, check account balance, etc. No doubt others will follow.

13. Gambling on the Internet continues to grow

As computers and software become more sophisticated, Las Vegas-quality video games will be playable from the privacy of your own computer. Any winnings can be transferred to your offshore account.

14. Print will not die!

The death of print has been predicted since the computer. Over the next 5 to 10 years I do not foresee drastic reduction in print publications. On the contrary, they will probably increase.

15. Internet advertising will evolve

Current print promotion techniques will become the standard for successful advertising. Already, Internet promotions using sweepstakes, contests, free reports, newsletters and books are being successfully employed.

Direct Marketing Principles That Will Not Change

For most people, change is exciting. But it can also be scary. You can take comfort in certain direct marketing constants that will never change! Here's why.

- The basic wants and needs of people have always been the same. And, they will stay the same. In the future, consumers will continue to want what they do today:

    —more money

    —family security and safety

    —convenience—easier living

    —better health

    —more leisure time

    —travel

    —privacy

    —lower taxes

    —freedom from government

- Basics are crucially important. More so than ever. Direct marketing success, regardless of what "delivery system" is used, will continue to rest on *copy*, *product* or service and *offer*.

- All direct marketing success rests on correctly targeting prospects—the right audience.

- The basic rules of direct marketing success will not change. Even if we begin to live in space stations or on other planets!

- The best two books on direct marketing I ever read are *Scientific Advertising* by Claude Hopkins and *My First Hundred Million* by E. Haldeman-Julius. The first was written in 1927, the second in 1928. 76 years ago! The principles in these books still hold today. These principles will not change 76 years from now! Or 1,000 years from now!

- Two-step marketing is and will continue to be an excellent way to generate sales, both in print media as well as the Internet. Your offers succeed by getting more prospects to raise their hand before sending a letter selling the dickens out of your product.

- Futurists are wrong about the death of direct mail! Direct mail will continue to be the real workhorse of direct marketing. Other important media will continue to be:

    A. Print ads—magazines, newspapers, yellow pages.

    B. TV

    C. CD's

    D. Internet

Information will be available in many new and improved formats, including CD's videos, audios, software, etc. However, publishers can rest assured that books and other printed materials will *not* become obsolete.

Actions to take to best capitalize on future opportunity

As previously mentioned, you as a direct marketer can face the future confidently, without fear or anxiety. Why?

More than any other individuals, direct marketers are perfectly positioned to capitalize on the new trends. You already make a living directly touching the hot buttons of your prospects.

However, we must all think about our business in the proper way.

1. Identify the business in which you are engaged.

In doing seminars around the world, I always ask entrepreneurs in the audience this question:

"What business are you in?"

The answer to this question at first seems so simple and easy. But for most, it's the most difficult of all. The right answer can mean success. The wrong one failure.

You may have heard this classic story. The President of the Pennsylvania Railroad over 50 years ago when asked this question said, "The railroad business." This was the wrong answer.

The right answer is the transportation business. Had this been the answer, the company could have prospered by getting into air and other forms of transportation. Instead, the company went into bankruptcy during the 1970's.

When I ask publishers what business they are in, almost all of them say "book publishing." That's the wrong answer. The right answer is "the information business"! Why is this so important? Because fundamentally there is no real difference in the form in which you package information.

Tip: *Think about the fundamental nature of your business. Once you correctly identify this factor, you'll be in the top 1/10th of 1% of all businesses.*

2. Study human behavior.

Those who best understand psychology and human behavior will prosper. Being able to identify what makes people buy is key to direct marketing success. Some people seem to have an instinctive ability to relate to other humans. But the best ones, the real champions, study psychology. You can learn a lot studying people, especially your audience. However, I don't know of a better, faster way than through books.

Tip: *Read everything you can by these authors: Ayn Rand, Abraham Maslow, Nathaniel Branden, Albert Janov, Elizabeth Kubler-Ross, Thomas Gordon, Roger Callahan, and Wayne Dyer.*

3. Develop active listening skills.

Perhaps the most misunderstood communication skill - it's assumed we all know how to listen. But we don't do it well or naturally. What does the term active listening mean? Focused attention. Really hearing people express words, listening to inflections, and tone of voice.

As with all skills, active listening must be learned. It's not taught in any school of which I'm aware. It's so important, perhaps one day it will become part of all good education.

In case you are skeptical about its importance, consider this. How many people do you know who are good active listeners? I'd be surprised if there are more than 2 or 3. Of my close friends, I can only think of three.

Do you think you are a good active listener? Try this simple test. Ask friends or family to grade you from 1 to 100. Regardless of the feedback, you can improve.

Here is the reality. Unless you effectively learn to listen to your prospects' problems and desires, there is no possible way you can create the most desirable products or services to serve their needs and that maximize your profits.

Tip: *To be a good active listener, start today. Attend seminars. Read books. And practice, practice, practice, on a daily basis. Start with your family and friends.*

4. Continue to increase your knowledge.

The best way known is to read for at least one hour a day.

One of the most valuable tapes I ever listened to was Earl Nightingale 27 years ago. He said that if you read one hour a day on any subject for three years, you can master any topic. After five years, you will become a world expert!

Reading is the best investment you'll ever make in yourself. Why? You are learning from the distilled wisdom of the greatest minds in the world.

When one is busy, it's so easy to get away from the reading habit. We've all done it.

But I'm rededicated to the wonder and joy of reading. During my around-the-world trip, I read 19 books, 12 were non-fiction, 7 were fiction. I learned incredibly important things. For example, I discovered the two best investment books I have ever read: *The Investment Biker* by Jim Rogers and *The Warren Buffet Way*. I've changed my whole investment philosophy as a result.

The second best way to learn is in seminars. Attend seminars conducted by proven masters of their fields. I recommend you attend at least 8-12 each year. This knowledge you gain is the best investment you can ever make.

5. Develop the two-step marketing technique.

Run small lead-generating ads in print media and the Internet. Follow up with a series of sales letters that powerfully promote your product. Apply the techniques in this book.

6. Sell internationally.

The world can be your market! It's easy to sell internationally if you do it right. The fastest, easiest, lowest-cost, lowest-risk way to succeed with international sales is this.

Once you establish a successful product or service in one country, assign licenses to people in other countries.

Concentrate special attention on Europe, Japan, Australia, New Zealand, and the emerging markets of China, Malaysia and Thailand.

7. Test market on Internet, TV, CD's, and other emerging technologies.

Remain curious and aware. However, always stay a step behind new technology. Don't bet the ranch on any new trend. Unless you feel compelled to be first, let others be pioneers. Remember what happens to pioneers. They have many arrows in their backside.

8. Re-cycle previously successful advertising campaigns—done 10, 15, even 20 years ago.

Currently, I'm re-running ads which were successful years ago with amazingly good results. Remember, sales principles do not change.

9. Support direct marketing educational activities at the university level

These activities conducted not by academics, but by people who "walk the talk" and are masters of their topic in the real world. Currently, very little is offered in formal education for students interested in a career in direct marketing. How about a Doctorate of Direct Marketing! Wouldn't you like to hire one?

How will the 21st Century be Different?

Currently, most citizens throughout the world are subjected to burdensome government controls. However, governments can control its citizens only through:

- *Censorship*—The first thing all dictators need to establish. However, no government can effectively censor its citizens any longer. Happily, communication breakthroughs via Internet, satellite TV, fax and computers make it impossible.

- *Banking*—Power-hungry governments need complete access to the financial records of its citizens. However, banking can now be completely private so no government can discover what its citizens choose to do with their property.

- *Privacy of communication*—A key tenet of individual freedom, is now possible via encryption.

Because of the dramatic effects of human ingenuity, we're about to enter the most exciting period in the history of mankind. Why? The 21st century will finally result in "the triumph of the individual." The new technology and breakthroughs will make it simply impossible for any government to maintain control over its individual citizens any longer!

The net result: dictatorships cannot be maintained for very long. Entrepreneurship and free markets will exist as never before. Just imagine the standard of living truly free people will achieve.

Summary

Preparing this particular chapter has been a fascinating experience for me. I've gotten a lot of help from my friend, Jeff Groves, especially on the technical predictions. I've shared with you my direct marketing predictions, principles in direct marketing that will not change, and recommendations on what actions you can take to capitalize on opportunities. I hope you've enjoyed the journey.

What an exciting time the future holds for all of us!

Combine the results of the information age with this fact. The health and nutritional knowledge now exists wherein everyone will soon have the opportunity to live a lifespan of from 120 to 140 years.

In the meantime, together let's do everything possible to prepare. Perhaps the best thing to do is provide benefits to others through our enterprise while earning our just rewards.

How to Generate Great Ideas

Ever been stuck for a good idea? Perhaps you needed a good idea for a new ad. Or a new product. Possibly you've searched for a creative solution to a pressing personal or business problem. This chapter is dedicated to facilitating the process of generating ideas.

Ever wonder why some people seem to have a never-ending supply of fresh, new ideas while others have great difficulty? I feel humans are capable of far more ideas than we may realize.

Some say we use 5% to 10% of our mental capacity. I think they are wrong. I'd be surprised if any of us uses more than 2% of our capabilities. The potential of the human mind is far more awesome than any of the wonders of the world.

Actually, very little is known about the enormous power of the human brain.

The experts say we are just scratching the surface of that wondrous part of us, the mind, with over 5 billion brain cells. I know we are all designed to do far greater things. So, why settle for mediocrity?

In my 20's, I used to speak for fun before Mensa groups about the Objectivist philosophy. As you are undoubtedly aware, it's necessary to have a genius IQ of 148 or better to be a member of Mensa.

At first I was surprised that even with high IQ's, relatively few Mensa members I met had accomplished much in their lives. But then I realized a basic human trait.

It's *not the size of your IQ* that counts most in life. *What you do with what you have* is infinitely more important.

I'm convinced *certain actions* help trigger great ideas. The key is to *create conditions* which *help stimulate the subconscious mind.*

Undoubtedly, some actions I'm about to suggest you'll really enjoy. Others may make you somewhat uncomfortable. Give both kinds a try.

Here are my favorite ways to help trigger breakthrough ideas.

1. Vary your daily routine.

Doing the same things in the same way at the same time every day may feel comfortable. And that's the problem. You can be pulling yourself into a rut. Plus, it can be deadly boring.

To grow creatively, or in any other way, you need to test—go beyond your comfort zone. Go as far as you'll allow yourself to go.

A good place to start is to simply vary your daily schedule.

Try this. For one day, *reverse the order of activities*. What you normally do first, do last. Vary other portions of your schedule, i.e., when you read the newspaper, exercise, go to the post office. Take a different route to and from work.

After you do this for one day, try it for a weekend. Then a week. You'll be amazed at the result.

2. Start your day differently.

The most vulnerable time emotionally for all of us is immediately upon waking up. The emotions you have then tend to set the tone for the whole day. Negative feelings of foreboding, fear, and lack of confidence are commonly experienced. These come from the incredible number of negative messages we "self-talk" into our subconscious. Messages of helplessness and despair are also fed to us daily by the media. Plus, well-meaning friends and family contribute to negative messages in many cases. Mine included!

However, *all emotions come from the meaning we give* to events. Happily, this means we can at will create a positive emotional state simply by changing our self-talk. We can manipulate our mind. One way to create positive feelings is through *affirmations*. Here are a few of mine that will work for you as well because they are *absolutely true*. Try this. Say them out loud as soon as you awaken first thing in the morning. After each one, say *YES*!

- I'm a creative marvel.
- Nothing great or worthwhile ever comes easy, and I'm willing to do whatever is necessary.
- Because I'm unique in all the world, no one can be like me.
- I have the capacity to do anything I really want.
- Individuals have always made a difference in this world, and I can too.

Remember, great people who made a difference were all single individuals. They worked against great odds. They were ridiculed and often risked their lives, fortunes, and "sacred honor." Aristotle, Ayn Rand, Columbus, Thomas Jefferson, Jesus Christ, George Washington Carver, Charles Darwin, Galileo, Copernicus, Thomas Paine and John Hancock are but a few of them.

3. Take a walk, jog, ride a bike or swim a few laps.

The physical activity in solitude stimulates your brain in a special way. New ideas seem to come out of the blue.

4. Start keeping a journal.

Answer just two questions each day:

What do I want?

What do I feel?

You'll be astonished at the material provided by your subconscious. This activity is my favorite idea stimulator and invaluable psychologically. It helps keep me on track emotionally. Otherwise, I can easily slip into a disowned state. (I spent years "numb" from feelings, not at all conducive to being creative.)

5. The "improve anything" exercise.

Look around your room right now, wherever you might be. Write down as many products as you can identify in 2 minutes. Can you think of some ways to improve them? You've just opened up many possibilities with which you could start a great business!

6. Listen to music by Mozart.

One study has shown mental abilities improve by 10% just by listening to music by Mozart. My favorite piece of music in the world is Mozart's Concerto No. 20. The emotional state listening to it creates in me is overwhelming.

7. Model success.

Study the work of successful business and creative people, past and present. Learn from them. Model them, but don't copy them, which can be illegal. Instead, see if you can identify the essence of their success. Then work on doing what they've done, differently or better.

8. Subscribe to *Readers Digest*, *People Magazine* and *National Inquirer*.

Reading these often maligned publications is one of today's best methods of spotting new trends. It's amusing that while these are among the best written and read periodicals in the world, seldom do people own up to reading them!

9. Subscribe to *The International Herald Tribune*.

This newspaper helps give you a way of looking at the world from an international point of view. Americans, more than other people, grow up with an insular viewpoint, believing that if it's not U.S. based, it's of lower quality, unoriginal, and other such nonsense.

10. Subscribe to as many newsletters as your budget allows.

The most independent and clear thinking available in written form is found in well-written newsletters. Plus, you'll get what's missing in most newspapers and magazines: a point of view. Study topics on health, investing, privacy, and travel as a minimum.

A few of my favorite newsletters include:

Newsletter	Editor	Publisher
Dow Jones Theory Reports	Richard Russell	Richard Russell
Forecasts & Strategies	Mark Skousen	Phillips Publishing
Daily Reckoning	Bill Bonner	Agora Publishing
Privacy Report	Michael Ketchem	Dan Rosenthal
Hideaway Report	Andrew Harper	Hideaway Reports
Health and Healing	Dr. Whitaker	Phillips Publishing

11. Vacation outside the U.S.

I don't know of anything more stimulating than a trip to a fascinating foreign land. Bring plenty of note paper for the new ideas which will come to you!

12. Attend a seminar.

A workshop given by a master in his/her field will really get the creative juices flowing.

13. Take a millionaire to lunch.

When you are in the company of any really accomplished person, prepare some questions in advance. Make sure you listen far more than you talk.

14. Hire a row boat and go fishing.

There is something special and almost magical about the sounds and sights of water.

15. Listen to people "bitch".

The best definition of a successful entrepreneur I know is "problem solver." Listen to complaints carefully. Think through possible solutions. Solve the problems people complain about and create a great product or service that will make you very wealthy.

16. Write a letter to someone you love.

Expressing feelings of caring helps you access deeply held emotions. Often, ideas are "hatched" when you are in a peak emotional state. Plus, even if you don't get new ideas, it just feels really good to tell a loved one how you feel, which none of us does often enough.

17. Read some poetry.

I especially love Rudyard Kipling, Elizabeth Barrett Browning and 13 year old Mattie J.T. Stepanek. Better still, compose a poem. What beauty and inspiration is provided by a good poem!

18. Watch an emotional movie.

A good film can stir those emotions which provide a great environment for new ideas. Don't watch at home, but on a giant screen.

19. Strike up a conversation with anyone under 8 years old.

Children, especially before the third grade, are often phenomenally creative. They are free and uninhibited.

Sadly, by age 9 or so they begin to lose these beautiful qualities. By the time they become adults, their creativity is often completely stifled. I feel it's mostly because nearly everyone becomes discouraged, unchallenged, and bored with today's education. Plus the cumulative effect of all the discouraging messages.

20. Call an old friend you care about . . .

And with whom you haven't spoken for a while. Tell her or him how you feel about them and what their relationship means to you.

21. Eat a hot fudge sundae.

Remember how much fun it used to be to really enjoy one topped with real whipped cream without guilt?!

22. Buy 9 books and read them within the next 60 days. Select them from the following:

A. A biography of either Winston Churchill, G. Washington Carver, Milton Hershey, F. W. Woolworth, Thomas Edison, Andrew Carnegie, or Sam Walton.

B. *Atlas Shrugged* by Ayn Rand

C. *Economics in One Lesson* by Henry Hazlett

D. *Your Body's Many Cries for Water* by Dr. Batmanghelidj

E. *Ageless Body, Timeless Mind* by Deepak Chopra

F. *Ordinary Children, Extraordinary Teachers* by Marva Collins

G. *How I Found Freedom In An Unfree World* by Harry Browne

H. *The Precious Present* by Spencer Johnson

I. *Using Your Brain For A Change* by Richard Bandler

J. *Jonathan Livingston Seagull* by Richard Bach

23. On a sunny day, lie on a hammock, relax and daydream.

You will refresh your creative capacity in a special way.

24. Discover your hidden talents.

We all have enormous talents and abilities of which we are unaware. The best way I know to self-discovery is a series of aptitude tests. This costs about $500 at a company called Johnson O'Connor Human Engineering Laboratory. They have offices in most major cities. In my opinion, everyone would benefit enormously with improved self-awareness, including your children. I have learned much about myself, as has Bethany, my children, and key employees.

25. Go to a restaurant and eavesdrop on conversations around you.

It's amazing what great ideas you will get listening to what preoccupies others.

26. Hire a masseur or masseuse for a deep body massage.

In case you haven't been massaged professionally for a long time, if ever, you'll find it a lot of fun, healthy, and stimulating in dozens of ways.

27. Take a vacation unique to your past experience.

Experience completely new things. For example, if you've never done so, travel by bicycle, go hiking, ballooning, snorkeling, take a safari or cruise. Go to a golf or tennis camp. Visit a nude beach. Try something you've never before experienced.

28. Study a subject at a college or university.

Sign up for a class which interests you. Learning new things and meeting new people stimulate ideas in special ways.

29. Single out someone you don't know.

Introduce yourself, ask about their profession or business. Just listen. Resist discussing yourself unless you are asked.

30. Rent "Crazy People" . . .

. . . the movie starring Dudley Moore. You'll stimulate ideas and learn a lot about generating great advertising by watching uninhibited people in action.

31. Find the loveliest tree within a block of your home.

Spend some time really appreciating its wonder and beauty.

32. Start engaging in the hobby you've always yearned to pursue but haven't.

You'll have a great time and surprise yourself with how interesting the new people really are.

33. Plant some flowers and watch them grow.

There is nothing as magnificent in nature as budding flowers. They will inspire you.

34. Study old advertising.

Ads which ran 30-50 years ago are generally far better than most of what you see today. You'll get great ideas to use in your marketing, too, because human emotions never change.

35. Discover what products are selling in other countries.

You can easily replicate the success in your market area. If a product is successful in one country, there is a good likelihood it will succeed in other countries. This is the lowest risk method of generating new product ideas I've ever seen.

36. Visit someone in a hospital or prison.

There is something special you'll discover about yourself when you engage in this form of reaching out to another human being. Plus, the person will benefit from your visit in ways that will touch you deeply.

37. Walk on a beach.

Listen to the sea and daydream.

38. Go on a picnic with your mate or closest friend.

Just focus on having as much fun as possible.

39. Take off your watch and spend a day without it and resist looking at a clock.

As simple as it may sound, this can be incredibly difficult the first time. It's so easy for all of us to be a slave to time, rather than its master.

40. Play with toys or children's games alone, with other adults, or if more comfortable, with a child.

I feel we've deeply buried the child that still exists within all of us. Yet the childlike part is the most creative. That's why children can say things that can be super headlines, as they are free and uninhibited. Playing child games seems to bring out that quality in adults. Some consultants are having great success doing this with executive groups.

Some wonderful activities that can help put you in a creative, playful mood are:

- Blowing bubbles
- Molding Silly Putty
- Playing with yo-yo's
- Playing with slinky toys
- Putting puzzles together
- Painting a picture by the dots

Try one the next time you get together with friends. They'll have a great time, or really think you've "lost" it!

41. Study acting as a hobby.

There is something special creatively that happens when you play someone else. You must learn to "walk in their shoes," an essential for any great marketer who wishes to understand customers.

There is one great and simple way to accomplish this. Start a local play-reading group with friends. Here are some tips on how to do it.

Limit the group to 15 people. Read the plays in character, but don't memorize, which frees you of the burden of investing hours of time to do so. Have a meeting once a month, 9 months a year. Alternate houses each month. The host selects the play and casts the characters. Serve coffee and dessert at the end of the first act.

My group has had so much fun and learned a lot with really wonderful plays, including: *Harvey*, *Inherit the Wind*, *The Man Who Came to Dinner*, Greek tragedies, and *The Night of January 16th*.

Try as many of these tips as your comfort level allows. And you can stop worrying about generating great ideas. They will come—you can count on it!

How Many of These 17 Commonly Accepted Myths are Blocking Your Path to Real Success?

I've learned the hard way. Through a great deal of trial and error and measuring results, I've come to this conclusion. Most commonly held beliefs are erroneous.

In fact, I submit that 97% of "conventional wisdom" is wrong. Dead wrong. Conventional wisdom is mythology, by and large.

Because I consider it my responsibility to do all I can in this book to help you be a more successful marketer, this chapter is about correcting certain underlying premises without which no long-term success is possible.

To the degree any of us unquestioningly accepts this "wisdom," the results are always disastrous. Frustration. Unhappiness. But conventional wisdom is far more than incorrect. It's destructive to happiness and success. It often puts life itself in grave danger.

Ironically, the conventional wisdom we have accepted was taught to us innocently. Without malice. With no intent to harm us. Indeed, what adult figures in our lives passed along to us was simply the conventional wisdom they erroneously accepted in theirs. But the fact remains, 97% of what we learned from our teachers, relatives, and friends is often mythology.

The good news is that we have the capacity to re-examine and change all the ideas taught us regardless of source.

Perhaps our greatest human capacity is **our power to choose.**

It is our choice. We can continue operating our lives based on erroneous principles. Or we can change and adopt new premises which are more conducive to a successful life.

What exactly do I mean about harmful ideas? Here are 17 commonly held myths which can block anyone's path to success.

1. Selfishness is evil. Man's highest virtue is self-sacrifice.

The word selfishness is perhaps the most misunderstood word in the English language. It's important to define terms to clearly understand selfishness. There are two kinds of selfishness.

Negative selfishness is evil. That's when you ask others to sacrifice themselves for you. To give up a greater value for a lesser value. This is what liars and con men ask of others. The result is someone wins while someone loses.

> ***Reality:*** **The world cannot function without positive selfishness.**

Free enterprise literally feeds the world. But it doesn't work anywhere unless people exchange *equal* values. Successful entrepreneurs can only become rich when *both parties win* in their transactions.

Most people feel guilty, and therefore unworthy, about acquiring wealth. So they never achieve it. You cannot be wealthy and completely happy in your life until you fully grasp positive selfishness.

2. Most business people are a little bit shady.

This ridiculous idea is accepted and taught by many teachers, professors, parents, writers and politicians. T.V. and movie scripts usually portray the wealthy characters this way, i.e. J.R. Ewing, Cash McCall, *Wall Street,* etc. Plus, the manner in which the early American industrialists such as Henry Ford, John Wanamaker, F. W. Woolworth, John D. Rockefeller and J. P. Morgan are depicted in books is outrageous.

Reality: **Wealthy entrepreneurs cannot remain successful over time unless they have a good reputation and lots of people continue to trust them.**

While there is an occasional dishonest business person who makes headlines, 99.9% of entrepreneurs in America and the world are decent, honest and hard working.

3. Money is not important.

This is really nonsense. Notice that the people who express this myth do not have any money.

I don't mean to suggest that money is everything. For real success in life, *balance* is what we should seek. Balance between health, career and personal relationships is, in my view, the 3 main ingredients. However,

Reality: **Money is crucially important!**

This principle desperately needs adoption, especially in America. Instead, the majority use denial. They don't save or plan for the future. Americans are saving less than 3% of their earnings. They rank only number 7 in the world in savings according to *The Wall Street Journal*.

Here is what is happening today in America:

> Out of every hundred people, age 25—
>
> 66 will live to age 65
>
> 5 will be working for a mere existence
>
> 4 will be in good circumstances
>
> 1 will be wealthy
>
> 56 will be dependent on their families, pensions, the community, or government for the very bread and butter they eat

Imagine! In the wealthiest country in the history of the world, only 1 out of 100 really makes it!

But you can be that person! And when you accumulate sufficient wealth, you will have the greatest value that money can give you. Freedom! You will be in position to travel anywhere. Live anywhere. Change professions. Work or play.

If you haven't yet earned sufficient wealth, don't despair! It's never too late. I know people who became wealthy in their 60s and 70s. And even in their 80s!

4. The little guy can't make it big anymore.

So many go around muttering this myth. It's incredible. Many MBA students repeat this destructive idea which their professors taught them.

> ***Reality:*** **There has never been a time in business history with more opportunities for the little guy!**

Look at the facts. There are over 20,000,000 one-person home-based businesses. Over 70,000 new corporations are formed in the

U.S. each month. Most are small, one-person enterprises. Nearly all are started with little or no capital.

This is the age of the virtual corporation. If you haven't yet started your own business, don't delay. *Now is the time*!

5. To fail at anything is bad.

We are taught that even to fail a grade in school is a terrible thing.

Reality: **To be more successful, increase your failure rate!**

There can be no progress in life without what others call failure.

A child doesn't learn that he/she can be harmed by a hot stove unless he/she gets burned. If a young student takes a course, tries his/her best and fails, the course can be repeated. Nothing bad happens! It's the same in business.

Perhaps I've written more successful space ads and sales letters than anyone in the last 20 years. Here is what is less known. I've had 4 or 5 times more failures than successes. That's why to get to the successes, I'm willing to try all sorts of things that don't work. I learned to love my failures. Why? Because I learn from them! I consider my failure rate a crucial part of my or anyone's success process.

6. Fear of failure keeps many from starting a business.

Most universities, books and seminars in business advocate this myth.

Reality: **Fear of success keeps many from starting a business.**

Success in any business endeavor requires a belief in oneself. A high level of self-esteem.

However, by the time most of us are in the third grade we've accepted a destructive idea. Deep down we feel we're not good enough to succeed in a big way. To have material possessions like a mansion, a Mercedes, a Rolls Royce, a big wardrobe, and foreign travel. We don't really deserve all the material things life can provide us. We accept a have-not philosophy. And we proceed to live our lives with our hat in our hand.

You must develop a healthy self-esteem to really get rich. You must learn to feel worthy and good enough about yourself.

Two books which have been helpful to me are: *Psychology of Self Esteem* and *Honoring Thy Self*, both by Nathaniel Branden

7. To become successful, find a need and fill it.

Surely you remember the lesson well. You can rarely find a business book or university course, including Harvard Business School, that doesn't perpetuate this idea.

In the past, I've lost a lot of money trying to make this principle work. This commonly taught myth has undoubtedly caused more bankruptcies than any other.

Reality: **To become rich, find a want and fill it.**

People do not buy what they need. Never. Never. They always, always buy what they want.

To illustrate this truth, I often ask this question at my seminars. "How many people would like to have a Mercedes? Or Rolls Royce? Or Jaguar? Or Porche? Or Lexus?" Many raise their hand.

Then I ask, "How many need one?" No one raises their hand. Of course, the point is this. The only thing really needed is transportation, which can just as easily be provided in a used car.

8. Logic sells products and services.

Many business people create sales presentations or ads filled with irrefutable logic. But sales results are often disappointing or even non-existent.

***Reality:* Emotional appeals sell products and services.**

Nearly all human action is a result of an emotional action. Or reaction.

There has never been success in any great endeavor without emotion. The creation of a great product, company, cathedral, cause, group, church or skyscraper requires getting others emotionally stirred up enough to act.

To succeed in business, you must touch emotional "hot buttons" in selling your product or service. This is true both in personal sales or via direct marketing methods.

9. Lack of capital is the biggest obstacle to getting a business started.

This common myth, once accepted, defeats many before they ever start. People feel it's not possible for them to raise the necessary capital.

***Reality:* You can always find someone to finance your business venture.**

Raising money is simply not a problem. A well-thought-out business plan is the key.

Often you can test your ideas in a small way requiring little or no capital before going big. You can "bootstrap" your start in many cases. This is the method I've used several times.

However, if you still need capital, finance a small start. Here is the "secret." You must be willing to approach enough people to invest with you. Most quit too soon. They get turned down by 2-3 banks for example, get discouraged and quit.

You may need to talk with dozens of private investors, bankers, venture capitalists, and underwriters to get your idea off the ground.

However, if you do it right, I'm convinced you can finance almost anything! Let's think of something really bold, such as privately financing a space expedition. Providing you financially justify it, I'm confident the money could be raised.

Bottom line. In my experience, no matter how unusual, there is always someone out there who will finance your deal.

10. Business-to-business marketing is different.

One of the well-known direct marketing trade magazines once referred to me in an article as "one of the top 5 business-to-business marketers in the world." (Conventional wisdom uses the "business-to-business" phrase a lot, as you've undoubtedly noticed.)

The editor called me and asked my reaction. I thanked him for the well-intended description of my skills. However, I startled him when I didn't agree with the article's conclusions. Here is what I told the reporter.

> *Reality:* **There is no such thing as business-to-business marketing!**

The only thing that exists in marketing is communication with another person. A business doesn't buy anything. People do.

One of the biggest reasons I've been successful selling business products to business owners is precisely because I don't view the process as selling to businesses. Most marketers use what I call a "Business Boring" approach. I sell to people. *Emotionally.*

Remember this. Business owners are people first and foremost. With aspirations, feelings and dreams.

If you want to sell to business owners in a big way, take the business-to-business phrase out of your vocabulary. Appeal to people's human emotions. Then sit back and watch your bottom line grow!

11. Retirement is a worthwhile goal.

The American dream includes a carefree retirement at age 65 or younger, usually in a warm pleasant place such as Arizona, Florida or California.

Reality: **People don't retire to live, they retire to die.**

Conventional retirement is a huge mistake.

Here is what insurance companies do not tell you. On average, people who retire at age 65 live an average of only 17 months. Having personally lived in Florida, I witnessed the effects of this sad phenomenon on a daily basis.

However, those who keep working live an average of 19 years! Most people get much of their self-esteem from their work. We all need to be wanted and needed.

Plus, there are many other reasons to keep active in your business or profession. These include the pleasure of productive work and independence. The extra income can be very important as well, precisely because you will live longer.

So, if you want to live a longer, healthier life, don't retire!

12. Don't waste your time with unimportant, "small" people.

The biggest loser in life is any person with such a view of fellow humans.

Reality: **Every human being is important and should be treated with dignity and respect.**

There are no "small" people.

I've discovered there is no wasted energy in the universe.

Whatever energy you put forth toward others always comes back to you manifold. Sometimes psychically. Sometimes financially. But it always comes back to you.

Plus, all people with whom you come in contact have much more power to impact your life than at first you may realize.

13. Aptitude is important to achieving big success in life.

Many people fail to act toward big goals because they don't feel they have "it." It is thought of as superior aptitudes, such as I.Q., personality, skills and other "natural" talents.

> ***Reality:*** **Success is no more than 20% aptitude. It's 80% attitude!**

Differences between people with genius I.Q.'s and average ones are not nearly as important as attitudes. For example, many Mensa members with a 140+ I.Q. achieve little in life. Yet, many high achievers, writers, speakers and millionaires have an average or slightly above-average I.Q.

It's not what you have that counts. It's what you do with what you have. It boils down to attitude.

I used to hire people based on skills. Now I hire attitude. Skills can easily be learned.

14. Chronological age is important.

You hear it every day. "If I weren't so young and inexperienced, or old and tired with my best years behind me, I could have done it."

***Reality:* Age is mostly a mental state.**

I put people into two categories: "young" and "old." The young are focused on the now. And the future. The old dwell on the past.

I know people who are chronologically as old as 87 but are young by this definition.

I know a lot of young people who are "old." There is nothing more tragic than to be chronologically in your 30's and 40's, or 50's and 60's and to be dwelling on the past. These people are old, don't you agree?

In which category are you?

15. Don't ever take a job beneath you.

Many people of all ages would rather collect unemployment than take a low-level position. This is especially true with today's young MBA graduates, lawyers, etc., who can't get a job.

***Reality:* There are no jobs beneath you.**

If you have trouble getting a job or if circumstances such as a business setback or layoff require you to seek employment, take any job you can get.

Often, approached with the right attitude a job at the very bottom of a company's hierarchy leads to a fast rise to the top in responsibility, income and status.

16. Government officials are basically trustworthy.

Private citizens tend to give their elected officials the benefit of the doubt in all important matters.

Reality: "Power corrupts. Absolute power corrupts absolutely." —Lord Acton.

I agree with Will Rogers who said "No American is safe as long as Congress is in session."

Throughout the world government officials are not worthy of your trust. If you want to be as free as possible, here is a simple formula that works. Leave others alone. As an entrepreneur, avoid highly regulated businesses, keep a low profile and have as little to do with government as possible.

17. To be a successful entrepreneur, you must try to please everyone.

This is a formula for failure that is absolutely fool-proof!

***Reality:* To be a successful entrepreneur serve a niche market and forget the rest.**

When I ask business people, "Who is your market?", guess what most say? Everyone!

But there is no product or service that everyone wants.

To be successful, become a *niche marketer*. Understand and focus your efforts on the mind set of your particular prospects.

For example, in marketing to entrepreneurs, I purposely divide my target audience in half. My message is highly appealing to self-reliant people who want to be more independent, free, rich or otherwise improve their lives. Those who want someone else, such as the government or a rich relative, to solve life's problems are not attracted to my message. And this is how I plan it.

Accepting any or all of these 17 new realities into your life will make a huge difference.

Let me know how you progress.

How to Make Your Company An Everlasting Success

This chapter is designed just for you. It's aimed at an entrepreneur who truly wants to build an extremely profitable company. A business which remains successful forever.

To succeed in a big way, of course, you *must* attract first-time customers. This requires a saleable product. But rarely can a single product sustain an entire business for long. You must also have follow-up products resulting in *repeat business*. Direct marketing jargon for this is a good "back end." Why?

It's nearly impossible to survive and prosper with a single product, with one exception. You market a product which requires renewal or replacement. It's well known on Wall Street that one-product companies have the highest mortality rate.

Therefore, *before* you begin marketing any product or service, have your back end in place.

Do not make this common mistake. Start out with one product. Get some sales. Realize you need more sales. Then frantically search for other products to sell your customers. You will lose valuable time and sales which can never be replaced.

To attain a successful outcome, first you must think through the desired result.

Therefore, here is how I recommend you think about your business. Create a mental picture of an ice cream cone! I call it the "ice cream cone theory." (I have a very scientific reason for the name—I love ice cream!)

Regardless of the kind of business in which you are engaged, the principle I'm about to discuss applies.

To make this clear, let's look at a hypothetical situation. Let's say you are an information marketer of products directed to the niche market of CPA's and accountants. Here is what your cone might look like:

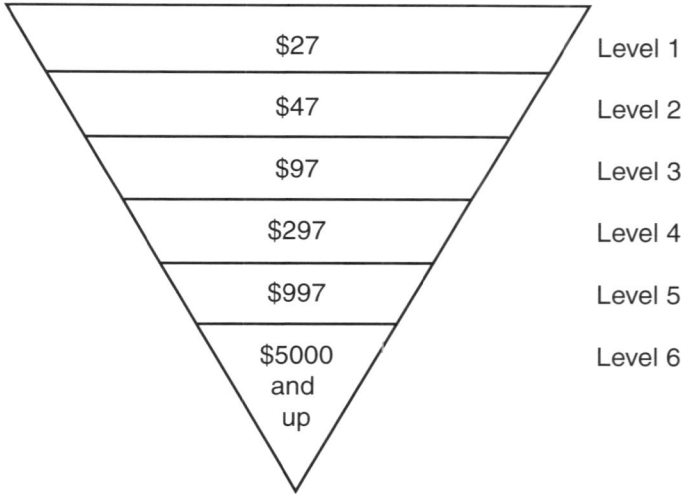

Ice-Cream Cone Theory

Products in our ice-cream cone could be as follows.

Level #1. A special report entitled, "7 Secret Ways to Legally Cut Small Business Owners' Taxes to Practically Nothing!"

Notice your cone is widest at the top. You want to capture as many people as you can at this stage.

Clearly, your first product is the most important. Otherwise, you won't get a second chance to make a first impression. So your goal should be to **astonish the customer!**

Make sure your product quality and packaging are more than what the customer expected. Then your customer will be very receptive to other offers. Why? Because trust has been established by how satisfied the customer is with the product and service. Trust is the key to any long relationship which can last a lifetime.

→ ***Important!*** *Stay within your niche. Do not make the common mistake of entering an entirely new market.*

Level #2. This product is a 6-cassette audio album of a one-day seminar on exactly the *same* subject as the book, "7 Secret Ways to Legally Cut Small Business Owners' Taxes to Practically Nothing!"

Level #3. This product is a two-video package which captures a live presentation on "Tax Saving Secrets You Should Reveal to Clients Without Being Asked."

Level #4. This product is a 2-day seminar "bootcamp" entitled "Secrets of Maximizing Profits From Entrepreneur Clients." (Notice all products are clearly related.)

Level #5. This product could be any one of the following:

- A day of consultation
- An advanced 3-day seminar on "Getting Rich With Your Accounting Practice"
- Daily rate for services as an expert witness in tax cases

Level #6. This is a minimum annual rate retainer for a growing small company, or monthly billings to a public company in need of extensive services.

Your very first task in building a great business

Let's assume you are at the point where you have an effective sales message. Your delivery system can take the form of an ad, sales letter, card deck, Internet, radio, TV, etc. New customers are being attracted profitably.

Most of the time you will begin the customer relationship with the Level 1 product. Of course, new customers can begin at any level. The future with any given customer completely depends on the level of satisfaction derived, beginning with the first product.

I can't stress it enough. It's crucially important to earn your customers' loyalty. You must provide at least what you promised.

Your goal ideally should be to **indelibly impress the customer. Give more than expected!**

Accomplish this and you'll always stand out where it counts. In the mind of your customer. You'll be head and shoulders above the competition. Surely you are aware how few companies give you as much as you expect. Let alone more.

Most people do not understand this simple principle. To become rich, you must live up to your promises. Indeed, do everything possible to exceed them.

Instead, many businesses look for shortcuts. They deliver as little as they can get away with. Then they charge as much as possible. This simply doesn't work. Customers soon discover this ploy.

Long-term success is built upon your *reputation*. There are simply no shortcuts to doing your job well. But the extra effort pays off. For everlasting success, ask yourself this question daily: "What can I do to increase my service?" Then take the actions required to do so.

After doing the right job in Level 1, amazing things will begin to happen for you. Many customers will become friends and clients for life! That's why the first product must not fail to impress your new customer.

The key factor in a successful business

Customer retention is the *key* to a successful enterprise. It's a true measure of how a company is doing. Yet, customer retention is not even known or factored in by more than 1/10 of 1% of companies. Surprisingly, the crucial importance of customer retention is not presently taught in business courses at the universities. Clearly, one of the most important principles in the business world is not widely recognized.

Customer retention can of course be measured arithmetically. Companies with 25% or less customer retention have to replace at least 75% of their customers each year. It's so expensive to find this level of new customers, the majority of these companies go under!

The successful companies retain 75% or more of their customers. That means they retain customers for a minimum of 5 years.

The mega-success level companies retain 90% of their customers. That translates to keeping the average customer for 10 years.

The profit differential between 90% and 75% retention is not a few percentage points. For example, it can be 5 times more profitable to retain a customer for 10 years than for 5 years!

The numbers tell it all.

Businesses in America spend 5 times as much money finding new customers as they do keeping existing ones. This is a huge mistake. What is your policy?

You should focus more effort and resources on selling to existing customers. Why? It's 4 times easier to sell to existing customers according to many experts. Customers already know and trust you if you have done the right kind of job.

There are really only three ways to improve any business:

1. Attract new customers through sound marketing;

2. Really work on quality and service to keep them; and

3. Sell more to existing customers.

A great deal can be learned from looking at examples of successful companies who have excellent back-end programs, and who also focus on existing customers.

Let's look at some outstanding companies who have achieved high customer retention rates:

Gillette Razor. Always on the lookout for methods which provide improved ways to shave, this company has a unique business formula. They are willing to invest in advertising and promotion. Their razors are sold at a low price just for a chance to provide one of the strongest back ends in businessæthe blades! Of course, their profits are earned on this built-in repeat business.

Dell Computer. Started in the college dorm room of Michael Dell in 1986, this company became the first in history to go from $800 million in sales to $2 billion in one yearæ1993 to 1994. They were innovators in many areas.

They direct market computers on a volume basis. Dell was the first company to position computers as commodities. But where they really shine is in customer service. They are the only company that you can call who will gladly help you solve a computer problem, whether or not you are their customer! Is it any wonder their customers are loyal?

Honda. On average, automobile companies lose over 50% of their customers each year. There is poor customer loyalty. Honda is different. They have a unique strategy resulting in a customer retention rate of over 70%. There are two reasons for this:

1. Fewer service problems because of a better made car.
2. Unlike their competition, they put a program in place to upgrade the same customers who buy Honda's into a more deluxe car in their product line, the Accord.

GEICO (Government Employees Insurance Corporation). This company retains customers because its basics are right. They provide insurance at competitive prices. They also give good service. They do not have a high-cost sales force, as do competitors. Marketing is done by direct mail.

Sees Candies. In my opinion, the finest confectioner in America. They maintain an unbeatable formula of handmade candies, high quality and reasonable prices. And excellent service. Their customers are fiercely loyal.

McDonald's. Even if you are not a big hamburger fan, you can respect this firm's strategy. While recently the company has experienced some setbacks, with few exceptions, they continue provide high-quality products, fast, courteous service and reasonable prices. A time-tested formula that is unbeatable. Adult customers and children, especially under 12, are very loyal.

Victoria's Secret. Starting out with a single store specializing in lingerie, it's now a chain of hundreds of stores. Plus, a tasteful catalogue is responsible for a healthy mail order business. Its customers demonstrate their loyalty by their ever growing repeat business.

Brookstone. Another retail store which has become a successful chain. Frequent catalogue mailings continue to generate healthy profits to its loyal customer base. Their customer retention rate is very high, over 90%.

JS&A. A well-run mail order business which began with high-tech products such as calculators, watches, computers, bread makers, air cleaners, etc. Today, my friend Joe Sugarman also markets via TV infomercials. His "BluBlocker" sunglasses, which have become a stunning international success, have a built-in repeat business factor when glasses need replacing.

Your Most Valuable Asset

Every great, well-managed business cherishes one thing above everything else: **their *database of customers.***

Many poorly run businesses, even with the help of today's computers, do not carefully maintain a customer database which is accurate and complete.

It's true whether you operate a retail store, restaurant, distributorship, professional service, or mail order company. How effective you maintain and nurture your list of customers will often determine how successful you'll be.

Mail to your customers often—at least once a month. Otherwise they start to forget you. Properly handled, your own customers are always the most responsive mailing list you will ever find. Renting someone else's mailing list and mailing to them can also be profitable, but not as productive as yours.

When your customer list exceeds 10,000 or so, you can create a new profit center. You can *offer your mailing list for rental* by other direct marketers offering quality, non-competitive products.

For many years, my mailing list consisting of over 500,000 buyers generated net annual profit from list rentals in the $500,000 to $750,000 range! List rental income is a large source of profits for professional direct marketers.

How to market "back-end" products

There are numerous ways to successfully sell follow-up products to your customers. Some may be obvious. But I will offer other unique ones that probably would not occur to you. Here are the techniques I found work best:

1. *Build repeat factor into the product itself.* This may be the best approach of all. Plus, it usually costs little or nothing extra. For example: a razor that requires blades; consumables (food or vitamins); a book, newsletter, or loose-leaf service that needs frequent updates; cosmetics, equipment that needs fuel or batteries; an annual membership club, etc.

2. *Insert offers in outgoing packages for related products.* When customers receive a smartly produced product from you, they are highly receptive to other offers. (For a unique method of launching a newsletter without a penny of investment, see my book 'Magic Words That Bring you Riches'. Several readers and self-publishers report huge success modeling this approach.)

3. *Insert your offer in other companies' outgoing packages.* You can often arrange to insert an offer for your product with companies not competitive with you. The financial arrangement can be your paying a fee per 1,000 outgoing packages of e.g. $100, or 10 cents each.

Or a split of sales, such as 50/50. If you are dealing with a quality company, their customers may be receptive to your offer. Of course, you must test to see what type of products in which your offer will work best.

4. *Send a well-written sales letter* to your existing customers offering the new product. In most cases, this will be your most effective method.

5. *Telephone or fax existing customers* informing them of the new product.

6. Add information about the new product to your *Internet website*. Follow up inquiries with a sales letter. Yours just might be one of the many products offered on the Internet which will really take off this year.

> **Actions to take:**
>
> - Develop the back-end approach to build a very profitable company.
> - Capture and stay in your niche.
> - Employ direct marketing techniques.
> - Develop quality follow-up products.
> - Put a strategy in place to sell them
>
> You can't miss creating a company which will be successful forever!

How to Create a Successful U.S.P.

A short sentence or phrase which sums up the main benefit of doing business with a company or primary product is often referred to in marketing terms as a unique selling proposition (USP). The term USP was originated by a famous ad man Rosser Reeves nearly 50 years ago.

Big success in business necessitates having a powerful USP.

However, few entrepreneurs direct enough attention to their USP. Of course, that's a big reason most are unsuccessful.

I will show you how to create a strong USP for individual products as well as for a company.

Perhaps the safest formula to a golden USP is one which *demonstrates value*.

The secret to creating a powerful USP is often contained in the *offer*.

When you prepare a value-driven offer or company summary, doing business with you can become almost irresistible.

I call effective marketing selling "dollars for dimes". Everyone wants to get value for their money.

Most people fail because they do the opposite. They try to sell "dimes for dollars". This doesn't work. People feel they are not getting value and won't buy.

When your company and its products represent a a real bargain, you have a marketing edge which is unbeatable.

A few years ago, consumers tended to spend money more freely. This is probably due to job insecurity and retirement concerns so prevalent today.

That's why bargain hunting has become very popular. Observe how rich people will admit shopping in discount or used clothing stores, etc. It's now even become fashionable to be frugal.

Therefore, offers and businesses, which are based on providing real value, often find a ready market almost instantly.

When a business attempts to sell "dimes for dollars", of course this does not give the perception of value.

The typical entrepreneur usually follows this sequence. He/she creates a business offering products and services. An untested, arbitrary price is established. Little thought is given to making the company and product USP compelling.

I've seen many excellent products that could have succeeded quickly die because of a weak USP. In many cases, another more alert entrepreneur picks up these companies and products at a bankruptcy sale. After repositioning them and creating a new USP, the new company experiences big success.

The successful marketer creates a USP that sizzles before launching a company or selling a product.

Examples of successful USP's

Let's examine some successful USP's. Some of them go back 50 years or more.

Many of the USP's continue to be used today. And they are just as strong as when they began.

Study the concepts behind the USP's which follow. This exercise will pay big dividends for you. Why? You will get many ideas for your company. And remember, ideas as such are not copyrightable. You can freely use the essence of them for your own purposes.

4 books for a dollar

This single concept created by famous copywriter Maxwell Sackheim was responsible for launching Book-of-the-Month Club. BOM is the world's largest book club because of it. Many other book clubs, including Quality Paperback, Doubleday, and Fortune have modeled their marketing on exactly the same or similar USP.

Hamburgers 19¢

The McDonald brothers started a new trend in the fast food business with this simple offer. Ray Kroc bought them out and continued building McDonald's with the theme of quality low-cost hamburgers.

The *Wall Street Journal* reported McDonald's is returning to its original USP of low-cost hamburgers at a reduced price. Interestingly, McDonald's management, with the support of a majority of its franchisees, is returning to its original USP as the most effective way to combat increasing competition.

Buy One—Get One Free

A huge success was built on this USP by the Mary Carter Paint Company (you got one free can of house paint with every one you purchased) during the 1950's and 60's. (Later the company got into financial difficulties due to over expansion in other unrelated businesses.)

This USP has built many companies in the past. Can you use this time-tested offer to create a USP for yourself?

Do-it-Yourself Incorporation

This USP is responsible for the success of one of my former companies—The Company Corporation (TCC). When I started TCC in 1972, you had no choice but to go through a lawyer and pay $300 to over $2,000 to incorporate a new company. TCC changed all that and made it possible for anyone to do it themselves. This revolutionized incorporation in America. When I sold the company in 1991, I had over 120,000 clients who had incorporated through TCC. I was their marketing consultant for several years. Today the TCC has over 250,000 clients.

Bargain Vacations

Club Med was founded in Europe and began with a unique and simple USP. A bargain vacation village. All meals, sports and social events were part of a single package price. No extras are charged. You don't need to carry around money. Rooms were not fancy, more like a barracks. And people continue to flock to Club Med wherever they open villages throughout the world. However, in recent years, they changed their approach aiming at a more affluent market. This new positioning has met with mixed success.

Pizza delivered in 30 minutes or it's free

This unique USP by founder Tom Monaghan changed the pizza business. This single idea is largely responsible for the enormous success of Domino's Pizza, with thousands of stores in the U.S. and several other countries. The USP has been imitated throughout the world.

Home of your dreams as low as $10,000

Bill Levitt single handedly changed America's suburbs forever with this USP. IN the 1940's and 50's Levitt built entire communities using mass production methods. The villages were called Levittown. For the first time owning your own home, formerly a dream, was now affordable for many people.

Today's successful developers use variations of this USP with, of course, inflation-adjusted pricing.

Brand New Ford $900!

Henry Ford sold new automobiles for under $1,000 for the very first time in the U.S. Ford's USP was made possible due to mass production techniques used in his factories. Interestingly, Ford also put in the first 8=-hour day for his workers. His pay was $8.00 for 8 hours, a high sum then. My father, later a restaurateur, was one of his employees, working as a machinist from 1919 to 1921.

Vitamins and minerals derived from living foods, not synthetic chemicals produced in a factory

I helped GreenPower, a supplement company in Holland, create this USP. This company's products came onto the market in 1997 using direct marketing techniques. GreenPower is now one of the largest multi-national companies in Europe.

An MLM company with quality and prices competitive with the best retail stores.

Cosway, a Malaysian company, has the most powerful USP I've seen in multi-level marketing. Quality and pricing which match, and often better, the best department stores. Plus, a great marketing plan.

Most MLM companies in my opinion have products which are way overpriced. Because consumers are extremely intelligent, they eventually discover this. An then the company starts a downward spiral and ultimately fails. Perhaps this is precisely why MLM companies often have a negative image.

Cosway is completely different and enormously successful. Started in 1979, they have over 70,000 distributors in Malaysia. They sell numerous brand name products, including cosmetics, vitamins, jewelry, appliances, gifts, etc. Their annual turnover exceeds 100 million dollars. They are now going into the Philippines, Brazil and Chile.

Sunglasses which protect your eyes

My old friend Joe Sugarman, who previously found the mail order firm JS&A, created a huge success with sunglasses called BluBlockers.

You may have seen Joe's TV infomercials, which are a great example of how testimonials can be used effectively.

The USP behind these glasses is a lens which protects the eyes from the sun's harmful ultra-violet rays at an affordable price. Several million pairs have been sold at approximately a $50 price point and are now available in certain retail stores.

A unique daily calendar

Many companies produce pocket calendars. The most successful one that has both a good product and an effective marketing plan is Day-Timers. Day-Timers' USP promoted via mail order is a better way to organize your time, a goal shared by every executive.

A privately run prison

Increased crime and overcrowded, high-cost prisons have created an unusual business opportunity for a company with a well thought out USP.

Corrections Corporation of America (CCA), a publicly traded company, has been extremely successful in contracting with state governments to build and operate prisons privately.

CCA is able to reduce states costs of maintaining prisons, while earning a profit. What a difference entrepreneurial solutions can make!

Slash legal costs

People are worried about the possibility of getting sued, and with good cause. The U.S. has become by far the most litigious society in the world with over a million lawyers in private practice.

Prepaid Legal Systems turned these fears into a business opportunity. Their USP is simple. You pay a small fixed monthly fee. For this you are protected. Should you need legal counsel or help in fighting a lawsuit or suing someone yourself, you will know exactly what your costs are, compared to the potentially ruinous costs of litigation with such a plan.

Audio tapes which inspire

Everyone likes to be motivated and inspired. Nightingale-Conant has becomes the largest mail order seller of audio tapes in the world with a unique USP.

They offer inspirational tapes based on the work of many of the U.S.'s top authors and speakers via mailing and through their catalogue.

Give away the razor at cost—make money on the blades

Gillette has one of the strongest USP's in the world. The company designs and offers the best razors it possibly can using the very latest technology. Then it sells these razors at cost. Of course, the only blade that fits is Gillette's. If you like the result you become a repeat customers.

This USP model has become the standard in the industry with Wilkinson, Schick and other following suit.

A strong USP is necessary, regardless of our marketing method. As you have seen by the examples I've used, several business types and marketing methods are represented. They include retail, service, mail order, MLM, hospitality, manufacturing and restaurants.

Looking at all these successes surely has your creative juices flowing. And there's more. I'm not done yet!

Step-by-step guide to creating a USP for your company

At my seminars, I work on helping attendees create a USP for their businesses.

Here is the best system I've found to facilitate the process.

After introducing and presenting the importance of a USP at a seminar, I assign some homework.

The USP homework assignment is this. Describe in 17 words or less the main benefit a prospect would derive from doing business with your company.

Tip: *Make a list of every possible way a person could possibly benefit from doing business with you. Write in a headline style. This is a good forerunner to selecting the strongest one.*

78 How to Turn Words into Money

The following day I work with attendees who want to share their homework. The purpose is to refine and improve the USP.

You can use this same process right now. Step back. Look at your business through the eyes of a potential customer.

Tip: *Your USP should answer this question. What is the biggest benefit and most unique benefit I, as a customer, will get from doing business with you?*

Work on refining the USP using the strongest, simplest words you possibly can.

You should use exactly the same process in creating a USP for a product.

An example of a successful offer

I completed a new audio tape program records at my seminar MAGIC WORDS THAT GROW YOUR BUSINESS. The retail price of the program is $317. Offering these audio tapes without anything special undoubtedly would produce some sales.

But watch what happens! I add an exciting free bonus. The offer's perception changes to a completely different deal.

It sizzles!

Here is the offer:

> You get every word of the seminar on tape, including questions and answers, plus a complete workbook with all handouts.
>
> If you order by the date shown on the order form (within 30 days) you also receive a free bonus. You get a complete written transcript of my renowned Self-Publishing Seminar, a $2,000 value absolutely free!

To summarize, you get the audio tapes, the written transcript of another seminar, total value at least $4,000, all for $317!

Notice how the "dollars for dimes" principle is employed! The offer is worth at least 10 times its cost! I'm sure you will agree this has more appeal.

Nearly everyone at all serious about marketing is probably going to order the program!

Quick Summary

To increase your success:

1. Create value in your company's USP.
2. Create value in your product's USP
3. Study successful companies to help model your USP.
4. Strive for a perceived value of 10 times cost ("dollars for dimes").
5. Use free bonuses which are related to help build value.

I look forward to getting a sample of your new USP's. Undoubtedly these will help you generate large sums of money.

But let's keep it all in perspective. Please remember what is all too easy for any of us to forget. Money is important. Very important. The only people who claim otherwise are deal wrong and usually broke themselves. But it's certainly not everything. *Balance between health, career, and your personal relationships is the key to a truly successful life.*

How to Create a Spiritual Company and Turn It Into a Multi-Million Dollar Success

"Spirit—An amazing or vital principle held to give life to physical organisms."
"Spirituality—Sensitivity or attachment to values."
—Merriam Webster

This chapter is about what is necessary to build a successful, profitable company in which you and everyone associated with it can take great pride.

If you do it right, owners, employees, customers, suppliers, and you will love your company!

What I'm about to reveal is known by perhaps 1/10 of 1% of the entrepreneurs of the world. The enterprises which employ even a few of the principles generate enormous wealth for their owners.

Yet, what I'm going to discuss is not understood or taught in any school or university of which I'm aware. I submit the main purpose of business is to **build value!**

When a company is built on sound principles, everyone connected with it becomes enriched. Both spiritually and financially.

The way to build value begins with your products and services.

You must offer a product and service your customers are so thrilled, so impressed with they are eager to buy more from you. Over and over again. Another big secret. Give more than expected. Far more. For example, providing unadvertised free bonus gifts can be a powerful strategy.

The goal should be to develop the highest possible level of: **customer loyalty**

The result is the "repeat business factor" which can run 80%–90%, even 95%.

Unprofitable businesses and those that fail have a very low repeat business factor. The reality is that most companies, including direct marketing organizations, fall into this category.

Short-sighted entrepreneurs often make this mistake. They often try to make a "killing" on the first product sold to a customer by cutting corners on quality and by not delivering a good value. It's almost impossible to make money or remain in business for an extended period of time using this approach.

Interestingly, conventional financial statements do not have any category for the repeat business factor. To my knowledge, business schools still do not teach its importance. Yet, the repeat business factor is crucial to the financial health of any enterprise.

> ***Tip:*** *Set up a control system that accurately measures the number and percentage of your repeat customers. Include a repeat business factor category on your financial statement so you and your staff are always aware of this vital number.*

Trust—the basis of all positive relationships

A key factor in building any great enterprise is the trust level within all your relationships with people. This includes employees, customers and suppliers.

In most organizations there is a shockingly low level of trust. Of course, there are good reasons for this lack of trust.

Many managers are not completely open, honest and above board with all the people with whom they deal. And, unfortunately, many business people manipulate and withhold important information. Others tell outright lies. Of course, such behavior destroys trust.

To build a great company there is one action you can take that helps to build trust better than anything else known. There is nothing simpler, nothing more powerful. It is the secret of great leaders. You must **keep your word!**

When you say you will do something, do whatever is necessary to make it happen. No excuses. When people know that as long as you are alive, what you say they absolutely can count on, they will be willing to perform miracles for you. They will move heaven and earth to make your company a huge success..

Keeping one's word is perhaps the *rarest* quality in all human behavior.

In recruiting employees and suppliers, again, you must find this powerful attribute. You must seek those rarest of individuals, those who **keep their word to you!**

I have spent much time during my career seeking such people. And I still do. I call it searching for eagles. It's been said:

"Eagles don't flock. You can only find them one at a time."

You can only build a great company with eagles! Not turkeys. Make no bones about it. Tell everyone about the only kind of people with whom you choose to work.

You must do what is necessary

You don't need people who when asked to do something whimper, "I'm doing the best I can." This all too popular phrase will lead you to failure, not success. It's not good enough for success. Virtually every time it's uttered a crucial task is not completed or done in a timely way.

You need people around you who have the attitude, "I will do *whatever is necessary* to make mutually agreed upon goals happen!"

A quick example. When I began Enterprise Publishing Company, I discovered the biggest complaint had by customers of competitive publishing companies was slow delivery. My first President, Joe Pasquini, was previously employed by Doubleday Books, the large New York publishing house. Joe explained they had over 10,000 complaints a month! This shocked me. Reason? People often had to wait as long as 6 to 8 weeks for the delivery of books they had ordered.

I'm sure when ordering by mail you've experienced the frustration of waiting an inordinate amount of time for your order. No doubt you thought twice about reordering from that company.

I consider order processing and product delivery part of the marketing process. Long delays in getting customers products was simply not acceptable to me in Enterprise Publishing. There is no excuse for long delays. I feel our customers who trust us enough to send in an order with advance payment deserve excellent service.

I established a simple policy from the beginning. Every order would be processed and shipped the same day as received. Not the next day. And certainly not the next week or next month, as some companies still persist in doing. This policy applies in my own company and in companies with whom I consult or in which I'm a partner.

Treat your employees with dignity and respect. Our warehouse employees have always been treated as a very key part of our marketing team. When hired, of course, they were told about our policy. Because in direct marketing, order levels fluctuate greatly depending on how many ads or mailings are being utilized.

That sometimes means working until late at night or even the wee hours of the morning to process that day's orders. Our employees do not go home until the orders are shipped. Does this policy sometimes inconvenience our employees? Of course. But everyone involved agrees it's worth it when the impact on customer relations is experienced.

Our customers are astonished with the quickness of delivery! Frequently orders taken on the telephone and sent UPS are received within two days!

Which customer, ours who got their order within two days, or a competitor's who waited 60 days, do you think is likely to reorder again and again? The answer is self-evident.

Interestingly, our employees feel proud of being with a company that treats customers in a manner represented by this small but important example.

What qualities to look for when hiring employees

When I first started in business I looked mostly for *job skills*, as do most employers. However, I discovered this was not the solution to finding employees who would perform like eagles.

Then I discovered the solution. I started

Hiring attitudes!

The key to successful recruiting is hiring the right attitude. With an exceptional attitude, virtually any skill can be learned.

How do you find the right attitude? A job candidate's attitude is revealed if you ask the right questions. Your job in interviewing is to become a good **active listener!**

Active listening is the least understood part of the communication process. Yet, it's equally as important as speaking or writing, perhaps more so. My father used to say, "You have two ears and one mouth for a reason. You should listen twice as much as you talk."

When conducting a job interview, ask open-ended questions. Then, listen carefully and make notes.

Examples of questions which help reveal attitudes of prospective employees are:

- What are the 3 most important books you've ever read in your life and why?
- Who were the 3 most influential people you've ever known?
- Of what job-related achievement are you most proud?
- What do you consider the prime purpose of any business?
- For you, how would you describe the ideal job?
- If you were supervising an employee who isn't doing their job, how would you handle it?
- How would you describe the ideal employer?
- How would you describe the ideal employee?
- Where would you like to be career-wise in five years?

These probing questions will be a big help to you in choosing employees. Of course, before asking them, be sure to indicate there are no right or wrong answers. Plus, it's important to state the information is strictly voluntary. Rarely does a prospective employee decline to answer. If they do decline, this in itself tells you a lot about how open he or she is. This may be important to you.

Once employees join you and come on board, a great way to facilitate taking responsibility quickly is to *empower* them. One of the best ways I've found is to give every employee the power to spend up to $100 of the company's money to correct any customer complaint or problem. This shows employees the value you place on customers by putting your money where your mouth is.

What do you do if an employee is not working out?

The best way I've ever seen of putting it is: **Hire slow. Fire fast.**

This may sound harsh. But it's actually the most humane way to manage employees.

For years I did the opposite. I'd hire fast, often on impulse, sometimes without even a probing interview. I didn't check references and previous employers, which was a big mistake. When I discovered the employee wasn't working out, I tried my darnedest to change them. Of course, you can't change anyone. People can only change themselves when they so choose.

It's far better to take your time in hiring. Nothing is more important in your company than hiring the right people. Always hire on a 90-day probationary period.

When a mistake is inevitably made, bring the person in right away. Talk with them and tell them it's not working out. They usually know it too. Let them go quickly and as gently as you can early on. It's never easy to let someone go. But it's much tougher later on.

How to compensate employees

The best way to compensate anyone is to give them a "piece of the action." This provides incentive, which all humans need.

There are various incentives you can provide that are terrific motivators, including:

A. An outright gift of shares of stock in your company.

B. An option to be rewarded with shares of stock when mutually agreed goals are met.

C. A % of sales.

D. A % of sales increase from one year to the other.

E. A % of profits.

F. A % of profit increase from one year to the next.

G. A generous pension or profit sharing plan.

H. Medical and life insurance benefits.

I. Benefits such as use of a new car, education expenses for children.

J. A paid vacation in an exotic resort.

K. Non-monetary recognition award at every opportunity. My companies are big givers of "eagle" awards! There are engraved plaques and statues which feature the American Eagle.

While some "piece of the action" examples may have pluses and minuses, I like and have used them all in various situations.

The bottom line: Smart entrepreneurs want their employees to become enriched in every way from the business. Reason? It's impossible to become really rich yourself without enriching others.

Thou shalt honor thy suppliers

In most companies' operations, suppliers are taken for granted. The only time many suppliers hear from their customers is in the form of complaints.

A really great business has leaders who treat their suppliers far differently.

If you want to really gain the cooperation of suppliers who always go the extra mile for you, again, **always keep your word to suppliers**

Pay their bill when you say you will, for example. Get the order and specifications to them when you say you will.

You just wouldn't believe how impressed suppliers will be because it's so rare! But impress upon them that if they want your continued business they must — you guessed it—**keep their word to you**

Tell people up front what you expect. Ask them if they are willing to work with you. If the printer has to stay up all night to get the brochures to you on the date they promised, he/she does it. They must operate as do you and your employees by doing whatever is necessary to keep their commitments.

Of course, not all suppliers choose to operate like this. You must get away from such people at once because with them you can't build a great enterprise.

But as you find suppliers who match your wants, honor them. You want to do everything possible to make them feel an integral part of your business "family."

I hold periodic parties for employees. I also invite suppliers to these celebrations. Engraved plaques are ordered for suppliers so we can present awards, i.e. (a) suppliers of the year; (b) eagle award for going the extra mile; (c) thanks, we appreciate you awards.

It's incredible how much these plaques which might cost $50 mean to suppliers. Remember, they seldom get any recognition. Many times when presenting the awards my suppliers have been so moved they start shedding tears!

The cookie-cutter factor

Another important element of a really successful growing business is what I call the "cookie cutter" factor.

Look for or create products, services and systems that can be easily duplicated. Create ads and mailings that can be used over and over again. License people in other countries to do the same thing and pay you royalties. The goal is as though you were putting dough in a cookie cutter and re-creating the same result over and over again. Anywhere. And everywhere.

Great businesses have built within them the "cookie cutter" factor. Examples include H&R Block, McDonald's, Microsoft, Dell Computers, Xerox and the Ford Motor Company. Businesses I've started, including Enterprise Publishing and The Company Corporation, all have the "cookie cutter" factor.

To summarize, in order to have a huge, mega success in your business, combine:

1. A quality product with an ever growing *repeat order rate*.

2. *Build trusting relationships* by setting an example, being open and keeping your word.

3. *Hire motivated employees* with a terrific *attitude* and *who keep their word*. They *must do whatever is necessary*. Ideal employees also must "buy in" to the idea that the purpose of business is to build value.

4. *Hire slow. Fire fast.*

5. *Recognize and honor your suppliers.*

6. *Look for and build in the "cookie cutter" factor.*

Result? You will have a growing, extremely profitable multi-million dollar business. You will be very proud of it. And both you and your employees will be rewarded beyond anything you can now imagine.

How to Generate Energy—
The Fuel of Success

Doctors around the world say the number one complaint expressed by patients goes something like this. "Doc, I have no energy. Can you help me?"

However, in my experience, the role of energy is virtually ignored by speakers and writers on the topic of success in books, seminars and newsletters.

I submit you the often overlooked role of energy is absolutely crucial to both business and personal success.

Here is a simple way of looking at this subject—a formula that illustrates how indispensable energy actually is:

$$\text{Talent} + \text{Energy} = \text{Big Success}$$
$$\text{Little Talent} + \text{Energy} = \text{Modest Success}$$
$$\text{Big Talent} + \text{No Energy} = \text{Failure}$$

Vitality is the motive power of marketing. All sales, no matter how you market your product, depend on it. However, vitality exists only when sufficient energy fuels it.

Just in case you have any doubts about how important energy really is, just think about this. Recall times tired and fatigued you tried writing copy. Or made a personal sales call.

You probably didn't do well. When your energy is low, it's almost impossible to perform at a high level.

As the late coach Vince Lombardi said, "Fatigue makes cowards of us all."

Factors that drain energy

No matter how much energy you have or can generate, there is always a finite amount. Therefore, it's important to reduce or eliminate factors that drain energy. Here are the major ones.

Stress

You have undoubtedly experienced stressful situations which seem to completely drain energy. You feel "wiped out". Completely eliminating stress may not be possible. Or desirable.

There are several actions you can take which reduce stress.

Negative people

Some people are constantly looking at the dark side of every situation. If your ideas are constantly "shot down" and you're told why a project or ad or business won't work, this becomes a huge energy drain. Unfortunately, many people, including employees, acquaintances, relatives and others close to us are experts at communicating negative ideas.

Poor diet

Consuming heavy, unbalanced meals, especially along with alcoholic beverages, is a drain on anyone's energy. A diet heavy in meat and fat and low on complex carbohydrates, fish, fruits, breads and vegetables makes you feel groggy and sleepy. The afternoon energy slump after a big lunch is commonplace.

Not keeping your word

You will experience mistrust from those to whom you've give your word. You'll also lower self-respect. This burns a lot of energy.

I consider management and staff not keeping their word to each other an epidemic in the business world. Is it any wonder in most organizations there is so little trust?

Boredom

The majority of people are not engaged in endeavors about which they are excited. Many activities lack challenge as well. The result is boredom, a major energy drain.

Being in the wrong job, profession, or business

The experts say 80% of the US population is engaged in a field not suited for them. Why? We tend to choose our life's work with less thought, facts and planning as, for example, buying a new car. Plus, there is little attention given to finding tasks best suited for each person's unique aptitudes and attitudes.

Being a control freak

This factor limits many entrepreneurs to a business size which will not grow and is destined to remain small. Many entrepreneurs are what I call "control freaks." Such people have great difficulty delegating. Instead, they try to do everything themselves. This is an enormous energy drain.

Depression

When you feel low, your energy level is expended far more quickly than otherwise.

Physical pain

When you are suffering from common ailments, such as a headache, backache, joint pain or chronic pain, your store of energy is quickly used up.

Disease

If your body's immune system is engaged in fighting disease of any kind, available energy drops quickly. Of course, many medicines also produce harmful side effects.

Self-criticism

Most high performers tend be far more critical of themselves than others. Being self-critical is a form of psychological punishment which seriously reduces both energy and self-esteem.

Physiology

Studies in neuro-linguistic programming conclude that 54% of our emotional state arises from our physiology. If you have any doubts about this statement, try this simple test for proof. Stand up. Round your shoulders forward. Look down at the floor. Shuffle very slowly around the room where you are now. Imitate the style of an old, arthritic man or woman. Within a minute or so you will be completely down mentally. Of course, your energy level will nose-dive too.

Negative self-talk

Perhaps the largest factor which drains energy quicker than any other is the way we silently talk to ourselves. Negative messages have been integrated into our conscious and subconscious minds. During our lives, we've all been exposed to negative messages which we often silently repeat. Sources of these words and phrases include parents, teachers, books and the media. For example, here are some of the messages my parents endlessly repeated to me:

"You can't do it."

"Money is the root of all evil."

"Who are you to think you can be rich and famous?"

"Be humble."

"Get a good, steady job, ideally as a pharmacist."

"Business is too risky."

"You are just a local boy."

"You don't have good contacts."

"The bank will say no."

You are truly a marvel!

With the many ways energy can be drained, it may seem miraculous anyone can be energetic. But they can. Your capacity to do so is truly a wonder of the world. Now I'm going to review many actions you can take to increase your level of energy manifold, at once.

Here is what you can do to immediately increase energy.

Dietary habits

Space does not permit a detailed look at diet. I'm of the view that everyone is a completely different metabolic type and has completely different needs. Some should eat a diet heavy in meat. Others become very healthy on a vegetarian diet. Most people, including myself, do best on a diet which is a balance of all food groups. A lot has to do with your genetic origin according to many nutritionists and physicians, such as Dr. William Donald Kelly.

However, these dietary factors are the same for everyone.

- Overeating is unhealthy, no matter what diet you follow.
- A low-fat diet (less than 30% fat) is best.
- Eat 3 meals a day.
- Don't eat between meals.
- Fresh, rather than processed, foods are better for you.

Drink lots of water. Recently I discovered the breakthrough work of a marvelous physician from Iran who has been studying the role of water on health for 17 years. His name is Dr. Ferrydoon Batmanghelidj. He's written a book entitled *Your Body's Many Cries for Water*. The book makes a convincing case that most people are seriously dehydrated, and that nearly every disease (including back pain) can be treated just with water. Plus, the cost is practically nothing. And your energy will skyrocket too. You should drink 18-24 glasses a day to get best results. You can get the book by calling 1-703-848-2333.

Supplements. Some doctors (and the FDA) say you can get all the vitamins, minerals and amino acids you need just from eating a balanced diet. Even if this were true, have you ever known anyone who eats a perfectly balanced diet? No? I haven't either, as such a person probably doesn't exist.

Plus, with the problem of seriously depleted soil, fruits and vegetables do not contain the nutrients of 20-40 years ago.

I'm a strong advocate of natural supplements, which I've been taking now for 21 years. The ideal is to take a balanced program that includes at least 90 known nutrients.

However, most supplements are sold one at a time. Taken in this way, they do you more harm than good. Because it's a problem finding a source of a good, balanced program, I'm currently involved with putting together a customized nutritional program depending on your diet. Stay tuned. I'll keep you posted.

Banish negative people from your life!

It's impossible to be successful and sustain a high energy level when everyone around us is constantly negative. You and I need support.

Therefore, difficult choices sometimes have to be made. You may have to find new friends. I found I had to do this. You also may need to stop spending significant time with relatives. And while I'm not advocating ending relationships lightly, in some instances, this may mean you'll need to leave a personal relationship.

Find an endeavor you love and turn it into a business.

Nothing can help generate and sustain energy better than a *passion* for what you enjoy doing most. Look for a field you feel so strongly about you would work in it for free. That's the way I feel about my work. There is absolutely nothing I can imagine I'd rather be doing, and to be so rewarded financially and emotionally is just icing on the cake.

Find the song you came to sing. Your enthusiasm will generate energy and sustain you through all the obstacles you will undoubtedly face.

If you dislike what you are currently doing, here is what I suggest. Get out of it as quickly as possible. You will not be able to generate the energy you need for an entire career. Plus, life is far too short to spend time on a career that you don't enjoy.

Get out of your comfort zone.

You cannot succeed big or sustain energy simply doing things that feel comfortable. High performing people achieve great things others do not for this reason. They are willing to take actions others fear or avoid precisely because they are not easy or comfortable. I submit the ideal way to operate is on the *edge of fear*.

This does not mean you take crazy actions or risks which scare you to death or have a low probability of success.

For example, make an appointment with that famous banker and ask for the loan you want. Or call the extremely wealthy investor to discuss your business deal. Or make that sales call you've been avoiding.

Dream big.

Then share the content of your dreams with other supportive people who can help you make it a reality. You'll be delighted at the energy you'll produce. Don't forget to include details in your dream about how you will help make this world a better place.

Keep your word.

Practice this simple act. You will unleash such a powerful and energizing force in your life it will amaze you. As stated earlier, most people may intend to keep their word. But in practice, it's rarely done.

All my professional life I seek friends, employees, suppliers, that keep their word. Trust is built in this way. Everywhere I go in the world, keepers of their word are the best people. They are extremely rare. But you can't build a great business, or for that matter, a great family, without it.

Here is how I feel you should operate. Let others know that unless you were to die, what you commit to doing will be done.

When others know you'll live up to your end of any deal, they will in turn be inclined to do so as well. And if they don't, stop dealing with them. You have to move on. But regardless of what others do, your self-respect will continue to grow.

Practice tough love.

Don't hold back. Tell people what you think and feel. But express your ideas in a hearable way. When those around you know you really do care about them, but will communicate what you want and expect in an atmosphere of dignity and respect, amazing things start to happen. The right kind of people will perform near miracles for you.

Plan your time.

A good system of time management increases energy if you do it right. Most people become exhausted by not having clear plans on usage of time. Instead, they allow outside factors, including distractions, interruptions and emergencies to direct their time for them.

I recommend a simple method I first discovered in a biography of one of America's most famous industrialists, Andrew Carnegie. Charles M. Schwab was a young employee working in Carnegie's office. One day having noticed Mr. Carnegie working frantically,

Schwab said, "I can teach you a simple method I guarantee will both increase your productivity while making you less tired at the end of the day. If you like it, you can pay me $25,000," a fortune at that time. "If you don't, you owe me nothing." Carnegie readily accepted the offer.

Here is the method. At the end of each day, write down the 6 most important things needing your attention most. Start the following day with the most important. Then proceed to the next important, crossing off the tasks in sequence. Do not allow yourself to work on anything else.

This is still the best method I have ever seen.

What do you think Mr. Carnegie did about the proposal? He happily paid Mr. Schwab the $25,000.

What about Mr. Schwab? He was named president of Carnegie Steel Co. in 1897. In 1901, he helped J.P. Morgan set up U.S. Steel Corporation and became its first president. Just two years later he personally bought Bethlehem Steel Corporation. Schwab credited his simple time planning system for much of his energy and success.

Hire slow. Fire fast.

Most entrepreneurs keep low performing employees far too long. They do the opposite to what I suggest. They hire fast and fire slow. I've done it many times, too. But you really can't change people if they don't take actions to change themselves.

It's far easier to completely change your approach. It's also better for your employees.

First carefully select employees. Start with well-written classified ads. (I see selecting employees as a marketing functionænot a personnel or administrative function, which is conventional wisdom in most organizations.)

Prepare a series of open-ended questions which cannot be answered yes or no. For example: "Would you mind telling me what are the five books you've read in your life that have had the most impact?" When your candidate answers, ask: "What is significant to you about them?" When your prospects answer, obviously, much about their mindset, attitudes and values are revealed.

Put every new hire on a 90-day probationary period, where at the end of which time he/she and you re-evaluate. If the relationship is not working at this point, deep down you know it. So does your employee. It's far better to terminate at this point rather than go on, as time only makes it more difficult to end it.

Hire attitudes, not skills.

While important to performance, skills can always be acquired. This is providing the employee has the right attitude. Conversely, a poor attitude cannot be overcome, no matter the skill level.

Share the wealth.

Create an atmosphere where you attract smart people with vitality and integrity as employees, partners and suppliers. Set up "piece of the action" terms for your colleagues. These can take the form of equity or a division of profits. These financial relationships will enrich others as you become wealthy. I've never met a multi-millionaire who did not make a lot of other people rich too. Remember, to get truly rich yourself, you must enrich others.

Exercise—but have fun.

Many people exercise out of a feeling of guilt. So they jog, join a health club, or do something else they feel they should but hate. This doesn't last long, as you can't sustain the energy. The experts say you are probably doing yourself more harm than good by releasing free radicals within you. So, quit doing what you hate. Instead, look for physical activities you enjoy. For example, walking in beautiful places near you; swimming at a picturesque beach, lake or pool; lifting weights; or playing tennis, badminton, handball, golf, basketball, volleyball, etc. Find what's right for you. Do it regularly and your energy will dramatically increase as a result.

Rest and relaxation.

A person with a high level of energy needs to take time to get proper rest. Find the number of hours of sleep where you function best. Some do well on 4-5 hours. Others need 8 or 9. My ideal sleep point is about 7 hours.

The secret of many high-performing people is less sleep and frequent naps. For example, Thomas Edison, Albert Einstein and Winston Churchill were nappers. I, too, occasionally benefit from short naps of about 30 minutes.

However, I prefer meditation. Years ago I even wrote a book on the topic, *Andocentric Meditation*, now out of print. Many scientific studies have confirmed vital signs, such as resting heart rate, improve and energy increases after meditating. A good way to learn an effective form of meditation is to take a class in transcendental meditation or buy a book on the topic, such as Dr. Howard Benson's *Relaxation Response*.

Keep a journal.

Each morning this is what I recommend you do. Write out the answers to these two simple questions in a private journal that will never be read by anyone else.

1. What do I feel?
2. What do I want?

Make sure to count you blessings, too.

My personal journal helps me do several things:

- Helps set the emotional tone for the day.
- Keeps me in touch with inner self.
- Contributes to my zest for life, and thus my energy level.

Suppose you don't take all the actions?

If you do take all the recommended actions, your energy level will undoubtedly soar. But here is more good news. You do not have to apply them all at once to increase energy. A few steps will make a big difference.

Just start out taking one or two actions. When you see for yourself the dramatic changes in your energy level, you can take one or two more steps. Then when you are ready, add more, etc.

10 Million Dollar Sales Secrets

Over time, I have spoken before CEO Clubs and numerous other groups around the United States and Europe. The topic: 10 simple ways to instantly increase sales. The feedback I received from attendees was so overwhelming I wanted to share that same information for the benefit of my readers.

I learned a long time ago that in preparing anything—manufactured goods, a book, a piece of software, a tape, a video, etc.—it's important to have a quality product. It's crucial. But the biggest job that we all face is to **get the sale.**

That's why a successful marketer must focus 95% of his/her energy on, **getting the sale**.

Direct marketing is the most efficient, powerful way that you could ever employ to get the sale in your companies.

The *number one task* of every healthy business is to *strengthen marketing*. I have never seen a business that can't benefit from a more powerful marketing program.

I don't want to be misunderstood. I'm not suggesting you replace your sales force, or your distributors, or your franchisees. Although in some companies that strategy is exactly what needs to be done. However, every situation is different.

Regardless of how you market and sell now, you can do it better employing direct marketing techniques. Because no matter what business you're in and how you're marketing now, better brochures, better sales letters, better space ads are going to have a tremendous impact on your activities.

Before going further, let's discuss success. Would you like a *success formula* that *never fails*?

You can *insure* your *success* with a discovery that is *foolproof!* It's a simple, 5-point plan that works every time.

1. The first thing you need to be successful in any business may be obvious. You need a **product** or service.

2. Next you need a **plan.** A strategy. Most businesses don't have a very sound or clear plan or strategy that everyone involved understands. This is where marketing comes into play.

3. To be really successful, mega-successful, you must have **passion** for what you're doing. If you don't love what you do, it's almost impossible for you to get bankers and customers and financiers excited about it. *You* have to be excited about it. Even if you're one of those rare one out of a thousand who can succeed in something you don't like, my recommendation is: *get out of it.* Because you're wasting your time. Life is too short. Do what you love and the money will follow.

4. The fourth thing you need to be successful is **energy.** Because there are going to be times that you'll need to work those long hours and long weeks. I'm not advocating workaholism. It's not healthy as a lifestyle. I've been a workaholic much of my life.

I've learned that the *key* is *balance*. One of the things I strive for now is balance between three factors: (1) *physical health*; (2) a *career that you love*; and (3) *personal relationships* that are meaningful. To me that's what success is really all about.

Energy arises from food. Adopt a low-fat diet. Lots of liquids, 8 glasses of water a day in addition to coffee, soft drinks, etc. I have a 90% rule. 90% of what I eat is nutritionally sound. I believe 10% is whatever tastes good. I believe 10% doesn't make any difference. Unfortunately, most people eat 90% "junk" and 10% good stuff.

The other thing that is important is that you have to feed yourself *positive mental foods*. Most mental foods that we feed ourselves in this society are negative. My full-page ads have about a thousand words in them. I was reading recently that there are about a thousand words that go through our minds every waking minute. 97% of conventional wisdom is wrong. Imagine the impact on all of us when those messages are the negative, erroneous, conventional wisdom that society feeds us. It's difficult to keep your energy level where it needs to be while listening to those negative messages. You must replace these messages with new ones.

5. The final thing you need to be successful is **action.** You can read great books and newsletters, go to seminars, learn the techniques. But *unless you act*, you can never be mega-successful. We know that at seminars what separates the mega-successful from the ones who don't achieve the kind of success they could is not acting on information. A Chinese general said a thousand years ago that having knowledge and not acting on it is the same as not having the knowledge at all.

What I'm going to share with you now is from my own experience, with my own investment in my own companies. It's not theory. It works.

I submit there's only one function of any business. And that is *to get and keep customers.*

There is no other reason to be in business. Now in order to get customers, the biggest media investment is no longer TV and press. Today it's direct mail, direct response space ads and telephone. According to *The Wall Street Journal* figures, it's $55 billion in direct advertising and telephone versus $19 billion in TV and press. Direct marketing is the way people are finding more and more as the better way to sell their product.

The main reasons that direct marketing gets the most dollars are:

A. *Sales calls cost at a minimum of over $400* (The number according to one CEO Club member is $600.) That's a lot of money to make one sales call. A sales letter costs about 70 cents. I'm not suggesting you eliminate your sales force, but if you can impact on greater sales in your company, including what you can do to help your sales force with some of these techniques, you are working in the right direction.

B. Another reason why direct marketing works so well is small tests can be done before committing large sums. If a test doesn't work, *you can change the offer*. You can crawl before you walk. What I love about direct marketing is I can run a small test of 3,000 pieces in the mail, or a small space ad, or a small two-step ad for a limited amount of money. If it doesn't work I can change it, again and again. When I find that winning formula, I can roll it out big. A lot of people look at my ads and say, "You must be a big risk taker." The truth is I don't like risks. I like to market very carefully. When I determine that it works in a small way, then I'm willing to invest in a larger way. The way I work is I run a $500 ad, or a $1,000 ad. Or I send out 1,000 pieces of mail for $600, $700 or $800, depending on what's in the mail package. When I get an indication of sales, then I go to 3,000; then to 5,000—25,000—100,000—250,000—1 million—2 million.

But I don't start out mailing in the millions. If you have a lot of money and are determined to waste it, make your test big. But most marketers don't have that problem. Direct marketing done correctly gives you the capacity to use a minimum amount of money to generate maximum sales.

C. It's the only form of *accountable advertising*. It's the only kind of advertising you can ever do where you can trace every dollar of sales to every dollar of costs. Major corporations using traditional advertising have no idea which advertising is effective. If you employ direct marketing you can tell exactly what works. I don't have to guess if this ad is working or not working, if this sales letter is working or not working, if this brochure is pulling. Did the addition of this brochure increase the sales from the previous brochure. It's the most financially controlled way to conduct marketing. What I'm interested in doing is getting the most sales for the least amount of money.

There are three ways to grow a business:

1. get more customers

2. raise the average sale

3. sell more to existing customers.

You could have a *pot of gold* at your feet underutilizing the greatest asset of all. Yet many businesses don't use it effectively. And that is your **customer list.**

The reason is: it's 16 times more difficult to get new customers than to sell to existing customers. Most entrepreneurs focus on getting new customers. I happen to be very good at getting new customers so for many years that's where I spent most of my time. Until I realized that the unmined gold is your existing customer base.

Avoid this costly mistake

A big mistake for business owners and CEO's in my view is to delegate the marketing function. The reason is this. If you accept the premise that the purpose of a business is to get and keep customers, isn't marketing the supreme dynamic umbrella under which all activities should fall? If that is the case, the owner should in most cases be the best instinctive marketer in the company because he or she has already gotten the business off the ground, has already marketed to bankers, relatives, customers, whatever it took to get that business going. There are exceptions to all rules. If you happen to have a dynamic marketing associate you might want to delegate that function. But 99% of the time it's a mistake to have someone other than yourself handle the marketing function.

Are you asking yourself the right questions?

Most clients we see say they have a conversion rate of leads to sales of 70% to 80%. When we actually look at the statistics we find that it's 20% to 30%. If you want to immediately increase sales, you work on converting your inquiries to sales. Your sales will double from the conversions.

What is a B.F.O.?

Huge marketing success is often the search for the obvious, what we call a B.F.O, a blinding flash of the obvious. Sometimes the best sales coups comes from doing something that should have been obvious but wasn't until it became obvious.

A *key* to *huge sales* success is *not price*. It's value. But you don't just get value accepted. *You must educate* your customer as to value. That's why your sales copy is so important. Your unique selling proposition (U.S.P.) must include why your product is of value to them. It's an educational process. Many of my friends assume their clients know everything about their business. The reality is you can't assume anything about your product or service. Your copy must educate your customers. Are you ready for the easiest, quickest ways you can impact sales? Here they are:

10 Simple Ways to Immediately Increase Sales

1. Write more letters to your customers.

I already mentioned this, but it's so important I want to expand on it. If you write to your customers twice a year, your sales will increase by 50% simply by writing twice as often. I have found that sales letters mailed to cold lists, people who have bought from competitors, mailing the same letter to that list within six weeks we get 50% of the initial response.

Just mail a successful letter more often and see your sales increase by 50%. It's a tremendous thing and a lot of direct marketers don't do this.

American entrepreneurs are the best in the world at direct marketing. But there's one area in which Europeans are better. Since their audience and niches are smaller, they've learned the value of repetitive mailings more so than Americans. In the U.S. the market is so large you don't have to pay as much attention as you do if the market is limited. The Europeans mail to inquiries on average 7 to 9 times before they give up. The average American direct marketer mails once, twice or three times and then stalks off into the night never to be heard from again. Big mistake.

Mail more frequently to existing customers. I have never seen a customer list that is over-mailed. Your customers want to hear from you. If you approach them properly with good mail—good, honest sincere offers—you cannot contact them often enough. Not long ago I read that John Henry Patterson, who started the National Cash Register Company in 1884, is the first person who started direct mailings to customers. He began mailing once a month, then once a week and then went on a hugely successful campaign mailing once a day, every day, for five months before a salesman called on the customer. By the time the salesman called, the potential customer knew all the benefits of the cash register. It paved the way for the sales people. The rest is history.

You want to mail as often as it's profitable. One of the techniques I use is to send the same offer on different color stationery. The first letter is sent out on white stationery, the second letter on primrose yellow stationery, the third letter is pink and the fourth letter is blue. The copy is the same. The average number of sales calls that have to be made in America by a sales person is five times. What makes you think you can send on letter and that's enough? In other words, if you need to make five personal sales calls, you have to send at least as many letters to get a successful response. Mailing more often is just a simple thing you can do to immediately impact sales.

> ***Tip:*** *If you are currently invoicing customers and are not now using fliers giving your customers the opportunity to buy other products at either the full price or a special price, you're missing a tremendous opportunity. You already have the envelope going out with the postage. By including a sales offer you're going to increase your sales without any additional sales expense.*

2. Include powerful letters with your brochures.

Have you ever sent a brochure to a prospect without a sales letter? Almost everyone has. But here's my recommendation. If you're going to mail only one thing, *forget the brochure*! Send a powerful sales letter instead. The sales letter filled with important benefits is the most important thing you send out. Why? Because it's the most personal connection you have with your potential customers. I'm not suggesting you drop sending out brochures. Just add a personal letter from you over your signature with the brochure to increase your sales enormously.

3. Better train your sales people to view every customer contact as an opportunity to sell.

Clearly that's obvious when you're dealing with a product inquiry. However, it may not be as obvious if someone calls to complain about something. In my companies we often get thousands of orders every week. Occasionally we get a few complaints. And what were the complaints about? 95% of the time a mistake was made at the warehouse and the wrong product would be shipped. We train our employees not to be defensive when a complaint is received. Instead, here are the magic words we learned to use: "If I were you, I'd feel the same way. Here's what we can do. We'll send the right product to you by overnight courier. You'll have it by 10:00 a.m. tomorrow morning. Will that meet your needs?"

Of course, the customer would be elated. And then the customer service person adds, "Before I hang up, would you like me to tell you about our special that we're running this month?" Over 50% bought! Instead of fearing complaints, any call, even a complaint, becomes an opportunity to sell.

Professional sales is not pressure. It's *helping customers fill needs*.

If you are in the retail business, train your people to avoid saying what everyone in retailing says: "May I help you?" And the common response is "No thanks. I'm just looking." That question terminates the conversation. Then the customer resents any attempts to build rapport, which is crucial to any sales environment.

I encouraged a recent seminar attendee, a retailer, to change their store policy to approaching customers with this question instead. "When was the last time you were in our store?" What that did was begin a rapport-building process.

That client increased their sales in their chain of retail by 27% in just two weeks! Why? The rapport built with the customer.

It's better to say "How may I help you?" than "May I help you?" because you're more in a service mode. This is a simple idea but an important and powerful one.

4. Offer free gifts and bonuses.

I've never sold anything than didn't sell better after offering free bonuses and gifts. Free is the most powerful word in the English language. If you're not using gifts and bonuses in your marketing operations now, your sales in many cases will go up 2, 3 and 4 times. Some of my clients sell books, 5 million dollar real estate, $3,000 computer software packages, etc. All have experienced huge increases in sales simply by offering a free bonus. It's amazing to some that adding a $15 Swiss Army knife as an inducement to buy a $3,000 product would work, but I assure you it does. Some of the other more popular free gifts are calculators, beer mugs, pens, and T-shirts.

5. Creative money-back guarantee.

If you do not have a money-back guarantee for your product or service, I urge you to test it. You will find your sales will dramatically rise. Because the biggest problem you have is always credibility. If I say to you, "If for any reason you are not 100% satisfied we will give you a prompt and courteous refund, every penny, that you have paid for our product or service". It eliminates that fear that everybody has that they're going to buy it and it's not going to be for them.

Here's what we find with guarantees. The longer the guarantee, the more acceptance you have. For example, a 30-day guarantee pulls more orders than a 10-day guarantee, 60 day guarantee pulls more than 30-day, a 6-month pulls more than 60 days, one year pulls more than 6 months. The longer the guarantee, the more people feel confident they can buy it and not be worried about losing their money.

6. Find more powerful U.S.P. driven reasons to buy your product. Be specific, not general.

For example, for someone selling a tax planning service, "Announcing a new way to save thousands of dollars on your taxes this year" is not nearly as effective as saying, "Announcing a new way to save $17,437 on your taxes." You see, what sells is *specificity*.

A *statement* not only *has* to *be true* in your marketing. It *also* has *to seem true*. Too much of American advertising, particularly the big agency type of advertising, is filled with exaggerated claims that are just too general. Third class mail is called "junk mail" and a lot of it is junk. It's filled with exaggerated claims. If you're specific and your statements are true, and in many cases using customer testimonials, you will have an edge over your competition.

7. Start a preferred customer club.

You undoubtedly are aware of the 80/20 rule. 20% of the people on any customer list buy 80% of the products. It's very easy and low cost to start a preferred customer club. You can issue a plastic card if you like and send a letter saying "Thank you for being such a loyal customer. Here is a preferred customer card. We appreciate your business. In the future, you will always get a discount". You want to encourage those preferred people to buy even more often. Because that's the lifeblood of your business. Start your club. It's very simple, powerful and inexpensive to do.

8. A well-written newsletter is a potent marketing tool.

I'm not talking about boring, boiler-plate "canned" newsletters that a lot of companies such as banks, insurance companies, accounting firms and lawyers publish. You're not going to help sales one iota with such publications. I'm talking about a newsletter that is *filled with useful information*, is written with passion, and is fun to read. This type of newsletter will develop a much more loyal bond with your customers. It's something to consider if it fits your operations.

9. Include "What do you think" cards with your products.

Again, it's easy and low cost to do. You take a card, like a postcard, or a short letter that says: "Thank you so much for choosing to be a customer of our company. We're always looking to improve. We would like you to tell us what you think about our products and services. Are there any suggestions or comments you have for us, because we are always interested in making it better for you, our customer."

Don't those words generate a feeling that someone really cares? The thank-you card asking for feedback is terrific. You'll also get *testimonials* that way from your customers who love your product. *Nothing is more powerful than words* from the hearts of your customers.

> ***Tip:*** *If you're not getting a lot of testimonials now unsolicited, there's nothing wrong in writing to your customers and saying, "We're revising our advertising. Would you be so kind to let us know what you think because we'd like to include some customer comments." You'll get back all kinds of comments. Hopefully 99.9% of them will be powerful comments that you can use.*

10. *Ask your customers for referrals.*

A terrific strategy to attract new customers is to ask for the names of 3 to 5 friends of your existing customers.

I have done this many times with a "member-get-a-member" club. By adding an inducement such as a discount certificate, you will increase the number of names you receive.

The most effective strategy to convert these referred names to customers is to write them a letter which includes these ideas: "Mr. William Johnson thought you might be interested in hearing about a service we provide him that has saved him money (or time, or increased revenue). If you have any questions about how we might be able to help you, too, please feel free to call. Of course there is no obligation."

These sales ideas are extremely powerful. Their *real beauty is in their simplicity*. You don't have to use complicated formulas. You will find you and your employees will be able to implement them easily.

How to Prepare Headlines that Make Money

As a reader who is interested in marketing, you are undoubtedly aware of the crucial importance of headlines. Whether your message "delivery system" involves a sales letter, print advertisement, Internet ad, card deck, TV or radio spot, the headline represents as much as 90% of the success of your offer.

Because headlines are so important, it's simply not possible to overemphasize techniques which can improve the process of preparing them.

Stuck for headline ideas?

This month I'll discuss one of the most powerful ways I know to prepare headlines. It doesn't matter what business you are in or what product or service you are marketing. The technique will improve your headlines.

Here's the procedure. Simply review current headlines, past or present, that have made money. Successful headlines are repeated over and over again, sometimes for more than 20 years! They are "controls" in direct marketing jargon, and they can be successfully recycled.

Because human nature stays the same, looking at advertising going back 70 years or so is prudent.

Older ads tend to have a higher percentage of good headlines than do present ads and direct mail, in my opinion. There were proportionately many more capable copywriters in the 1920's and 30's.

When you stop to think about it, there is an enormous need in this information age for excellent copywriters. If you're looking for a great, exciting and highly paid career for yourself, or perhaps a son or daughter, I don't know of a better one.

It's been said, "I've seen the future and it's in the past." This is certainly applicable to the art and science of preparing headlines.

I've prepared a special collection of headlines for you. The list is derived from ads in many industries promoting a variety of products and services. I've written 19 of the headlines on the list. The rest are by other copywriters, including John Caples, David Ogilvy, Claude Hopkins, Robert Collier and Maxwell Sackheim. Many headlines are so effective and famous they are considered "classics."

When preparing your headlines, don't simply copy the words verbatim. This may violate copyrights, which is unlawful and a basis for a lawsuit.

Instead, use the list of headlines to inspire ideas. Study these headlines. Strive to use the appeals in new ways. Make them better. One successful headline can lead to another. This gives you enormous possibilities! And, remember, the ideas behind the headlines are not copyrightable or legally protected, so you have a broad range of options.

127 Headlines That Made Money

1. They Laughed When I Sat Down At The Piano—But When I Started To Play!
2. The Secret to Becoming a Millionaire is Simply Using the Right Words
3. Do You Make These Mistakes in English?
4. How $7 Started Me On the Road to $35,000 a Year
5. Announcing the New Ford Cars for 19__
6. Magic Words That Bring You Riches
7. Order Christmas Gifts Now—Pay After January 20
8. Wage Your Own Personal Tax Revolt
9. I Was Tired of Living on Low Pay—So I Started Reading The *Wall Street Journal*
10. The Ultimate Tax Shelter
11. Get Rid of Money Worries for Good
12. Here's How To Have a Long and Healthy Life
13. What's Wrong In This Picture?
14. They Grinned When The Waiter Spoke To Me In French—But Their Laughter Changed To Amazement At My Reply
15. How an "S" Corporation Can Save You Tax
16. What Makes a Woman Lovable?
17. Can You Talk About Books With The Rest Of Them?
18. How I Became Popular Overnight
19. Wanted—Your Services as a High-Paid Real Estate Specialist
20. Do You Make These Travel Mistakes?
21. How I Raised Myself From Failure to Success in Selling
22. What Makes a Consultant Successful?

23. Stop Writing Letters the Hard Way

24. How I Improved My Memory In One Evening

25. How To Do Business Tax Free

26. Now! Own Florida Land This Easy Way . . . $20 Down And $20 A Month

27. How A "Fool Stunt" Made Me A Star Salesman

28. Thousands Have This Priceless Gift—But Never Discover It

29. You, A Millionaire Writer?

30. Free to High School Teachers—$6 to Others

31. How The Next 90 Days Can Change Your Life

32. 7 Ways to Break the Overweight Habit

33. The Lazy Man's Way to Riches

34. How To Do Your Christmas Shopping In 5 Minutes

35. Car Insurance at Low Cost—If You Are A Careful Driver

36. Who Else Wants A Screen Star Figure?

37. Imagine Me . . . Holding An Audience Spellbound For 30 Minutes!

38. It Cleans Your Breath While It Cleans Your Teeth

39. How to Win Friends and Influence People

40. Lose Ugly Fat—An Average of 7 Pounds a Month

41. How a Strange Accident Saved Me From Baldness

42. The Most Comfortable Shoes You've Ever Worn or Your Money Back

43. When Doctors "Feel Rotten" This Is What They Do

44. The Most Complete and Most Scholarly Dictionary in the English Language $17.50 . . . Publisher's List Price: $90

45. Find Your Own Tax Haven

46. How I Retired on a Guaranteed Income for Life
47. Slash Your Letter Writing Time by 80% and Write Better Letters
48. How You Can Get a Loan of $500
49. 161 New Ways to a Gourmet's Heart—In This Fascinating Book for Cooks
50. How a Man of 40 Can Retire in 15 Years
51. New House Paint by Du Pont Keeps Your White House Whiter
52. 10 Ways to Beat the High Cost of Living
53. How Investors Can Save 75% on Broker Commissions This Year
54. Free Book Tells You 12 Secrets of Better Lawn Care
55. How to See or Be a Lovebird
56. How to Feel Fit at Any Age
57. Sleeper Stock Bargains
58. How to Beat Tension Without Pills
59. New . . . A Cream Deodorant Which Safely Stops Perspiration
60. Here's a Quick Way to Break Up a Cold
61. The Eighth Wonder of the World
62. Why G.E. Bulbs Give More Light This Year
63. Play Guitar in 7 days or Money Back
64. How I Started a New Life With $7
65. Quick Relief for Tired Eyes
66. Thousands Now Play Who Never Thought They Could
67. How to Collect From Social Security at Any Age

68. Are You Ashamed of Smells in Your Home?

69. Tonight Serve This Ready-Mixed Chocolate Pudding

70. How to Stop Worrying

71. What's New In Summer Sandwiches?

72. How to Get Rid of an Inferiority Complex

73. I Lost That Ugly Bulge in 2 Minutes

74. The Most Amazing Shakespeare Bargain Ever Offered

75. You Don't Have to be Rich to Retire on a Guaranteed Income For Life

76. Who Else Wants a Lighter Cake—In Half the Mixing Time?

77. How to Get Your Cooking Bragged About

78. The Secret of Making People Like You

79. How to Make Money Writing Short Paragraphs

80. Double Your Money Back if This Isn't the Best Onion Soup You Ever Tasted

81. Can You Spot These 7 Common Decorating Sins?

82. Girls . . . Want Quick Curls?

83. To a Mother Whose Child is Three Years Old

84. Car Owners . . . Save One Gallon of Gas in Every Ten

85. Linen Napkin Luxury at a Paper Napkin Price

86. How $20 Spent May Save You $2,000

87. Have You Any of These Five Skin Troubles?

88. Will You Give Me 7 Days to Prove I Can Make You a New Man?

89. I Gambled a Postage Stamp and Won $35,840 in 2 Years

90. How I Made a Fortune With a "Fool" Idea

91. To Men Who Want to Quit Work Some Day

92. How to Get Enthusiastic Applause—Even A Standing Ovation—Every Time You Speak

93. The Deaf Now Hear Whispers

94. Hand Woven by the Mountain People of New Mexico

95. To Men Who Want to be Independent in the Next 10 Years

96. Free to Brides—$2 to Others

97. *Reader's Digest* Tells Why Filtered Cigarette Smoke is Better For Your Health.

98. Which of These Five Skin Troubles Would You Like to End?

99. If You Are a Careful Driver You Can Save Money on Car Insurance

100. Buy No Desk Until You've Seen This Sensation of the Business Show

101. Protect Your Corporation's Tax Shelter Status Without a Lawyer

102. They Thought I Was Crazy to Ship Live Maine Lobsters as Far as 1,800 Miles From the Ocean

103. Greatest Bible News in 341 Years

104. How to Have a Cool, Quiet Bedroom—Even on Hot Nights

105. To a Man Who is 35 and Dissatisfied

106. Have you These Symptoms of Nerve Exhaustion?

107. No Time for Yale—Took College Home

108. Great New Discovery Kills Kitchen Odors Quick!

109. I Tried 'Em All, But This is the Polish I Use on my Own Car

110. To People Who Want to Write—But Can't Get Started

111. Will Your Scalp Stand the Fingernail Test?

112. Owners Save 20% to 50% on Fuel With the G.E. Oil Furnace

113. The Tastiest Ocean Treat From Gloucester Plump, Tender, Juicy Salt Mackerel Fillet

114. Men Who "Know It All" Are Not Invited To Read This Page

115. How Two Natural Foods Can Prevent and Even Cure Cancer

116. To a $40,000 Man Who Would Like to be Making $80,000

117. Money-Saving Bargains from America's Oldest Diamond Discount House

118. You're Never Too Old to Hear Better

119. Throw Your Wax Can in the Trash Can—The New No-Wax Floor Is Here

120. How to Stretch Your Inflated Money

121. One Place Setting Free for Every Three You Buy

122. Who Else Wants a Whiter Wash—With No Hard Work?

123. Wanted—Safe Men for Dangerous Times

124. Instant Incorporation While U-Wait

125. How to Make Yourself Judgment Proof

126. Imagine Harry and Me Advertising Our Pears in *Fortune*

127. At 60 Miles an Hour the Loudest Noise in This New Rolls-Royce Comes From the Electric Clock

For a more effective presentation of your headlines, here are some reminders

1. Use no more than 17 words.
2. Use upper and lower case letters. Do not use all caps as they hard to read.
3. Capitalize the first letter of each word used.
4. Use classic typefaces, not newly developed ones. Times Roman is tough to beat.
5. Do not print in "reverse" type—white letters on black background. Use black letters on white or yellow background.
6. Quotation marks around headlines make them more noticeable.
7. Use words proven to be successful over time.
8. Include no more than one big idea.
9. When using a large photograph or drawing, lead with the picture and use a headline under it as a caption. Then begin your copy.

Secrets of a Profitable Ad

The fastest and most effective way to learn marketing is by studying actual examples of what works in the real world.

In this chapter I'll take you on a behind-the-scenes journey of a successful ad. I've never seen this valuable information published anywhere else. Therefore, what I'm about to reveal is exclusive and private material just for you.

Why would I share such precious information? As a loyal reader, we are soul mates on a similar path seeking marketing excellence. So, I feel comfortable treating you as if you are part of my family.

The product offered in the ad we will examine is my book, MAGIC WORDS THAT BRING YOU RICHES.

You may recall seeing the previous "control" ad for the book which was successful in the U.S. and several other countries. See Example A.

However, when I have an ad or mailing that is profitable, I'm always looking to beat results. Therefore, I'm frequently testing new copy against existing copy.

In addition, the previous "Magic Words" control ad was drawing book buyers who were not necessarily good prospects for follow-up offers (back-end offers). Because of the copy theme, many buyers

"It Amazed My Friend... I Said Two Simple Words. And We Were Escorted to the Finest Table in the Restaurant!"

And you'll never guess what they are! Yes, knowing the right words to say will get you everything you want in life

I'll never forget the look on her face. Pure joy!

You've surely had this experience. You make dinner reservations. You are taken to your table. Inevitably it's in a poor location. Usually by the kitchen where it's noisy. Or by the drafty front door. Oddly enough this often happens, even when the restaurant is not busy. It used to happen to me all the time. Until...

I learned the secret. Now I always get the very best table, wherever I go.

Certain Words Are Magic

One day while on vacation, it hit me like a bolt of lightning! Not only special treatment in restaurants, but all the good fortune I enjoy happens for just one reason. Because of words. Simple ones.

My name is Ted Nicholas. As a writer and speaker, I've been fascinated with words and phrases all my life. I've been refining these words for years. I've taught friends to say them. The same remarkable results happen to them.

No one is misled. Every word is truthful. Best of all, these words work for anyone.

Knowing the right words to say are responsible for my earning millions. As much as $3,500,000 in a single year. Getting 13 best-selling books published. Owning two, million dollar homes. Driving a new Mercedes convertible. And traveling throughout the world.

Think of it. I'm a college dropout. I began my career with no writing or speaking skills. No money. No contacts. No wealth, friends or relatives. No special privileges of any kind. And remarkable things have happened. All because of the power of these words.

Magic Words Will Change Your Life

I've decided to share these secrets for the very first time in my new book. I'll give you every word And to whom. In all types of situations which you face daily. You will then be in a position to enhance your life beyond what you've ever imagined. My book is called MAGIC WORDS THAT BRING YOU RICHES.

I know the book title sounds almost too good to be true. A little skeptical? I would be too if I were you. But don't worry. The "words" will work for you. You will be more successful at everything you do. And you'll enjoy it far more, too! Or the book won't cost you a dime! I'll reveal the secrets of how to:

- Always get the best table in any restaurant in the world. (And you won't have to spend one cent in tips to get it!) (page 11)
- Often get first class or business class seats on an airplane, even though you have coach tickets. (page 13)
- Have employers clamoring to call you with job offers, even during tough economic times. (This powerful technique never before in print anywhere will boggle your mind and get you the job you really want!) (page 19)
- Attract all the money you need for any business venture. (page 25)
- Approach an attractive woman or man and immediately interest them in you. (page 24)
- Rent a Mercedes automobile for the price of a Ford anywhere. (page 35)
- Find a great gourmet cook to prepare low cost meals for you. (page 39)
- Slash the cost of lodging in first class hotels by 50% or more. (page 21)
- Get invited to speak before any group you choose and enhance your career. (page 43)
- Receive free expert consulting help for your business. (page 38)
- Buy beautiful jewelry, including gold rings and watches at below wholesale. (page 40)
- Earn over $100,000 in the most profitable business in the world, and start it for under $600. (page 42)
- Find world famous people to speak before your group, free. (page 59)
- Attract the world's best employees using can't miss ads. (page 63)
- Get capable people to work for you for free. (page 67)
- Get free advertising by becoming a celebrity first locally, then nationally. (page 56)
- Obtain the U.S. rights to market best selling products from around the world for as little as $250. (page 77)
- Reduce or eliminate legal fees in both your business and personal life. (page 62)
- Buy valuable antiques at huge discounts. (Page 85)
- Get valuable, financial interests in other people's companies without investing one red cent. (page 89)
- Earn from $100,000 to $250,000 a year and more as a consultant by making an offer almost no one can turn down. (page 93)

A special section of my latest successful print ads and mailings is included that reveals powerful strategies which can earn you $500,000 or more on your products!

Sworn Statements

"I was Ted Nicholas' bookkeeper for 7 years and helped prepare his tax returns. To the best of my knowledge, everything he has stated in this message is absolutely true and accurate."

Gail Waterman

"I've known Ted Nicholas for some time now. He is a charming man and highly successful writer and speaker. However, when he told me of his new book I was more than skeptical that these ideas would work this side of the Atlantic. He gave me three ideas to try out for myself.

1. Within 4 weeks I found the best personal assistant I've ever employed.

2. I got free business advice that has already been worth over £20,000 to my company.

3. I now ALWAYS get the very best service at every restaurant I visit.

Now the book is ready I can't wait to work my way through his other great ideas!"

Mike Chantry
Hilite Ltd.
London, England

Special Offer

A limited edition of this remarkable book is ready. You are now able to reserve a copy while supplies last at a special price if you order now. To avoid disappointment, call immediately (800) 730-7777. Fax to (813) 596-6900 or complete the coupon below.

Money Back Guarantee

After you receive the book and examine it for 60 days, if for any reason you are not completely happy, return it undamaged for a prompt and courteous refund.

☐ Yes. Please rush a copy of MAGIC WORDS THAT BRING YOU RICHES, by Ted Nicholas at $19.97 plus $4 shipping & handling. I understand that if for any reason I am not delighted with the book, I may return it undamaged for a prompt and courteous refund.

☐ Enclosed is my check
☐ Please charge my:
    ☐ Visa ☐ MC ☐ AmEx

Card Number _____ Expires ____

Signature _____

Name _____

Address _____

City/State/Zip _____

Daytime Phone (if we have a question on your order) _____

Nicholas Direct, Inc.
Dept. 00-0
P.O. Box 877
Indian Rocks Beach, FL 34635

© 1995 Nicholas Direct, Inc.

Ad A

were not entrepreneurs or necessarily interested in becoming better marketers.

A completely new ad theme

So, I wrote a new ad with an entirely different approach. The goal was to both improve front-end sales response and improve results from back-end offers. The new ad is Example B.

The sales results from this ad are substantially better. In some magazines, results are *twice* as good as previously!

And, it gets even better. Much better. The back-end sales results are also stronger by a significant percentage. (The back-end sales, of course, arise from other product offers to the book buyers.)

The primary reason for improved sales of other products is because the new control ad *selects* a different buyer who is more in tune with other offers made by Nicholas Direct.

Now, let's turn to the key elements of the new control ad.

First, look at the lead or headline. By far, the most important element in any ad is the headline. The headline is 90% of the success of an ad. So, I place most of my efforts on it. The headline of Ad B is:

> **"The Secret to Becoming a Millionaire**
> **Is Simply Using the Right Words!"**

This headline appeals to virtually any entrepreneur. It makes no difference if he/she is a beginner or experienced. It draws immediate attention.

The previous control headline (Ad A) tends to attract consumers who are not necessarily entrepreneurs. Many are simply interested in getting a good restaurant table!

Experience with "Magic Word" buyers who purchased the book from Ad A shows that a small percentage, approximately 5%, purchase

Deeply in debt and worried about survival, I discovered ...

"The Secret to Becoming a Millionaire Is Simply Using the Right Words!"

You are 17 words or less away from a fortune! I'll reveal all the 'magic' words you'll ever need in my new book. Picture yourself earning several hundred thousands dollars a year. Work a few hours a week from the comfort of home, at a leisurely pace.

*Ted Nicholas
Self-Made Millionaire*

Certain words produce amazing results, as if by magic.

All you desire in life, including everlasting wealth, can be yours, depending on the words with which you express yourself.

Words have power. They can make you laugh. Or cry. Build a cathedral or skyscraper. Fight for your country. Who can ever forget the speeches of Winston Churchill, which stirred a nation. March for peace. Back your ideas with a million dollars. Or flock to buy your product!

That's why I call my new book MAGIC WORDS THAT BRING YOU RICHES.

I show you the exact words to enrich your life, financially and in numerous other ways, too. But, first, I want to tell you how I discovered the process.

At the age of 29 I had a wife and four children to support. Despite working 12 hour days, 7 days a week, poor decisions and bad luck left me $250,000 in debt.

I prayed for divine guidance. Suddenly a simple truth appeared to me. I was reflecting on the small successes I had in my life until that point in time. It hit me like a bolt of lightning! This discovery completely turned my life around. And it will change yours, too.

Different words produce different results! And it didn't matter whether they were spoken or written. As with the great truths, once known they seem so simple!

Then I began experimenting and testing different words and phrases communicating with people in business. I also decided to test a product idea in inexpensive classified ads.

The first ad cost me $90. It contained just 17 words. By mail I got back $360 in orders, all with payment! This may not sound like much, but to expand I

BONUS MAGIC WORDS - A special section of the book will also show you how to get the best table in any restaurant by saying just 2 magic Words. Raise all the money you'll ever need. Also have employers clamoring to offer you jobs, lease a Mercedes for the price of a Ford, fly first class for the price of coach, attract the opposite sex, and much, much more, all by using Magic Words!

Here is what you don't need.
- Money - I began with just $90.
- Office or equipment - A simple ruled pad and a pen at home is all I had to start with.
- A product - My book will show you exactly how to find a steady stream of hot products at little or no cost.
- Geographic location - My strategies work anywhere in the world, including a tiny village.
- Luck - My system does not involve any gambling or risk whatsoever.

found I could simply repeat the ad and multiply my success. I ran the same ad in numerous newspapers and magazines, over and over again. Within a short time my sales were $40,000 a month!

When I changed one or two words, I got vastly different response and profit. This blew my mind! Exactly the same thing happened in sales letters. I was determined to develop a vocabulary of simple words that I could scientifically prove were profitable.

I continued experimenting. I then ran my first full page ad. It cost $1,200. Sales from this attempt were $15,000. I repeated this ad in dozens of magazines. My sales soon exceeded $200,000 a month! And I still operated from the comfort of home.

Today, I have a lifestyle about which I always dreamed. I now live in a large penthouse in Clearwater, Florida. I view the Gulf of Mexico through windows 18 feet tall. My car is a red Mercedes convertible. We also maintain a lovely home in Switzerland, where we enjoy hiking and skiing.

The enormous power of Magic Words has made me a millionaire many times over. In 1991, I tried retirement. It lasted a few months. I found it wasn't all it is cracked up to be.

I looked for something else to do. I decided to share with others my discoveries in books and seminars. Since I don't need the money, I decided to give my secrets away Free as a form of charity. But I learned when people get something for nothing they usually place no value on it (this includes my own close relatives). So, I do the next best thing. I reveal my secrets at a cost anyone can afford.

Success based on Magic Words can be duplicated. You can do as well or better than me. Anyone who uses the words, and I mean anyone, can become a millionaire! Thousands of my readers have already become rich. A few of them are included below. And if you are sincere and apply yourself, you too will soon have all the money you desire.

What readers say.

"Ted's strategies earned me over $1,000,000 last year!" - Mike Enlow, Magnolia, Mississippi.

"Within the first 30 days after getting your secrets, I earned $30,000". - Francois Blot, Paris, France.

"Secrets I hope my competitors never see. If I could, I would ban this book immediately!" - Peter Hobday, copywriter, London.

"Ted Nicholas is one of the world's most gifted marketers. He's got the magic touch. Every moment I've spent with him has paid off enormously.", Bill Bonner, President, Agora, Baltimore, Maryland.

"...one of the greatest books on communications ever published. Absolutely must-reading for every person who wants more success, more money, more love, and more freedom." - Insiders Money-Making Report.

"Your book helped me earn £20,000 in the last 60 days. My son has also received 4 job offers in the last 3 weeks using ideas on page 15." - Mike Chantry, London.

IRON-CLAD GUARANTEE IN WRITING

I unconditionally guarantee this book in black and white. You can order this book risk-free, even if you are simply curious. If you fail to earn at least $900 per week within a 30-day period, in addition to your current income and while working no more than 12 hours a week at a leisurely pace, return the book and your postdated check/credit card authority will be returned to you uncashed.

However, I suggest you order at once. As much as I'd like to, I cannot guarantee the special low price more than 15 days. The book has been printed in the US under a special license arrangement with an independent publisher and this offer is a limited price test. The price will soon be substantially higher.

© 1997 Nicholas Direct Inc., 1511 Gulf Blvd., PO Box 877, Indian Rocks Beach, FL 33785.

---- **FREE TRIAL REQUEST** ----

TO TED: You seem so confident that you can help me make money so please rush me ____ copies of your book MAGIC WORDS THAT BRING YOU RICHES at $19.97 per copy (+ $4* S & H) on the strict understanding that if I am not delighted I can return the book to you before payment is due in 37 days. If I do, you will return my check/credit card authority uncashed and I won't owe you a penny. (* $8 Canadian $12 International.)

On that basis here's my order and postdated payment.
❏ Here is my check for $23.97 made out to Nicholas Direct Inc.
(Postdated for 1 month + 7 days (37 days).
❏ Charge my ❏ Visa ❏ Mastercard ❏ Amex (37 days after receipt)

Card Number..Exp. Date............

Signature..Today's Date...........

Name...

Address...

City...

State.....................................Zip..............

FAX YOUR CREDIT CARD ORDER TO 1-813-596-6900 OR MAIL THE COUPON TODAY TO:
TED NICHOLAS, NICHOLAS DIRECT INC., DEPT. , 1511 GULF BLVD., P.O. BOX 877, INDIAN ROCKS BEACH, FL 33785.

Ad B

back-end offers the first time made. While sales are profitable at this level, a significant percentage increase in response multiplies profit.

Of the buyers of the book from Ad B, 12% are buying back-end offers, an improvement of 140%! And 10 times more profitable! So the success of the ad has been greatly multiplied.

The role of the pre-headline

Pre-headlines can help set the stage for the headline. In this instance, I wanted to craft a phrase setting up a human condition to which everyone can identify, while *helping to dramatize the solution* contained in the headline.

The resulting pre-headline, "Deeply in debt and worried about survival, I discovered . . . " strikes a hot button. In our credit-dependent society, everyone tends to worry about mounting debts and the related problems caused by them.

The subhead includes important benefits

Copy within a good ad elaborates upon the big promise made in the headline. This process can begin in the subhead.

> ***Tip:*** *After the headline and whether or not you use a subhead, always start with your most important benefits first. The big danger of "saving" benefits until later in the copy is this. You may lose the prospect too soon as he/she may stop reading. Of course, once this happens, your chance of selling the product is lost.*
>
> *On the other hand, benefits to the reader practically compel reading the rest of the copy.*

Look more closely at the four sentences of which the subhead is composed:

1. **You are 17 words or less away from a fortune!**
2. **I'll reveal all the "magic" words you'll ever need in my new book.**
3. **Picture yourself earning several hundred thousand dollars a year.**
4. **Work a few hours a week from the comfort of home, at a leisurely pace.**

Every one of these sentences is strong enough to be a headline. Don't you agree?

Begin the body copy with a powerful first sentence

Now let's examine the body copy.

A crucially important part of any ad or sales letter is the *opening sentence*:

> **"Certain words produce amazing results, as if by magic."**

Don't you feel a pull to read on?

Look at the second sentence:

> **"All you desire in life, including everlasting wealth, can be yours, depending on the words with which you express yourself."**

This sentence was created to dramatize the enormous power of words in our lives. It's another way of expressing this profound truth: "The pen is mightier than the sword."

The third paragraph amplifies further the unique selling proposition (U.S.P.) of Magic Words.

> "Words have power. They can make you laugh. Or cry. Build a cathedral or skyscraper. Fight for your country. Who can ever forget the speeches of Winston Churchill, which stirred a nation. March for peace. Back your ideas with a million dollars. Or flock to buy your product."

In the fourth paragraph, I introduce the product being offered, which is, of course, the book MAGIC WORDS THAT BRING YOU RICHES. The product in a good ad should be made the "hero" of the ad, a process which begins in paragraph five.

> "I show you the exact words to enrich your life, financially and in numerous other ways, too."

Become a storyteller to hold attention

At this point, I switch to one of the most powerful copy techniques known ? I *tell a story*!

Public speakers, too, have long known the power of telling stories to drive home a point. The audience can be held spellbound by a good storyteller like Bill Gove, Zig Ziglar, or Robert Schuller. The same is true in writing copy for an ad or book.

Everyone loves a good story. But one caveat. Make sure stories you tell are absolutely true. Otherwise, they don't ring true. If your stories are not believed, you will immediately lose whatever credibility you have built with your prospect.

Here is how I introduced a story in the Magic Words ad.

> "But, first I want to tell you how I discovered the process."

The actual "rags to riches" story unfolds in subsequent paragraphs (see Ad B) until near the top of column three.

Relate the story to the prospect

Then I reveal what the reader is most of all really interested in. I answer the question, "What's in it for me?" I show the discovery I made can be *duplicated* by those reading the ad.

Prove it

To prove this claim, I refer to others who've successfully used "Magic Words".

At this point, testimonials are introduced. The power of testimonials cannot be overstated. The actual words from the hearts and minds of users of your product are one of the most powerful marketing tools you can employ.

A guarantee with power to double sales

Here is the guarantee in full.

> **"I unconditionally guarantee this book in black and white. You can order this book risk-free, even if you are simply curious. If you fail to earn at least $900 per week within a 30-day period, in addition to your current income and while working no more than 12 hours a week at a leisurely pace, return the book and your postdated check/credit card authority will be returned to you uncashed."**

This money-back guarantee contains two proven techniques to boost sales.

The first is a promise of extra income of at least $900 within a 30-day period.

The second part of the guarantee has the power to boost sales by 200% over a conventional money-back guarantee. While there is more handling involved and a longer waiting period to get paid, it's well worth it when you can double sales.

Photo caption

Please note that my name as author in the photo caption includes the words "self-made millionaire". This is very important as a connection is again made with headline theme.

Tip: *Reminder. Always caption every photograph used in an ad or mailing. Probably 75% of ads I review in magazines and newspapers have no caption whatsoever. The producers of such ads assume readers can figure out the purpose of the photo when it is often difficult or impossible.*

Boxes are used to set off important copy points

The first box contains important elements taken from Ad A under a subheadline offering a bonus:

> **BONUS MAGIC WORDS**—A special section of the book will also show you how to get the best table in any restaurant by saying just 2 Magic Words. Raise all themoney you'll ever need. Also have employers clamoring to offer you jobs, lease a Mercedes for the price of a Ford, fly first class for the price of coach, attract the opposite sex, and much, much more, all by using Magic Words!

In the second box I used a sub-headline which provides answers to questions had by every entrepreneur. I prepared them in such a way as to pique curiosity.

Here is what you don't need.

- **Money—I began with just $90.**

- **Office or equipment—A simple ruled pad and a pen at home is all I had to start with.**

- **A product—My book will show you exactly how to find a steady stream of hot products at little or no cost.**

- **Geographic location—My strategies work anywhere in the world, including a tiny village.**

- **Luck—My system does not involve any gambling or risk whatsoever.**

The all-important order coupon

The most important parts of the order coupon are the first sentence and a repeat of the guarantee.

Please note that unlike most order coupons, there is plenty of room for the customer to complete name, address and credit card information.

Tip: *Always complete order coupons yourself. Do this before running ads n any publication. You will be able to correct a common mistake: not allowing enough room for the customer to write. This error always reduces response, by as much as 75%.*

Quick summary of tips

- Don't hesitate trying completely new copy themes.
- To improve back-end sales, make sure your ads target the right prospect.
- Devote 90% of your effort on the headline.
- Test a pre-headline.
- Always caption photos.
- Use boxes to set off important copy points.
- Tell an interesting story.
- Test a hold-your-check-until satisfied guarantee.

I trust you've gleaned many tips from this rare behind-the-scenes look at a successful ad. Freely use the techniques. And enjoy the increased profits from your advertising.

33 Secrets of Successful Sales Letters

For 99% of my readers who engage in direct marketing, sales letters produce most of their sales and profit.

Sales letters, not space ads, card decks, TV, radio, etc., have traditionally been the real "workhorse" of direct marketers. Except for obvious differences such as envelopes, virtually all the recommendations herein also apply to e-mails.

However, most sales letters can be vastly improved. The result would be higher sales. A lot of potential money is being left on the table.

Because there is much room for improvement, the opportunities to earn huge profits from good sales letters are greater for you than ever before.

In this chapter I've put together rules to help remind you of the key points. I call them the "Sales Letter Success Rules." Each of them has been tested and proven. Here they are.

Sales Letter Success Rules

1. Preparation sequence for best results

Prepare your sales letter in this sequence:

    (A) Envelope

    (B) Order card

    (C) Letter

    (D) Brochure (optional)

    (E) Lift letter (optional)

Most people prepare the sales letter first and order card last.

2. Use a "teaser"

On the envelope, think of a teaser as a headline. It must be compelling. Otherwise, the envelope will probably not be opened. There are many ways to prepare teasers. In an e-mail, the teaser should be your subject line. The safest approach for a powerful teaser is to present the strongest benefit of your product.

3. Use the back of the envelope

Marketers most often waste a very important sales opportunity by leaving the back of the envelope blank. Many times prospects look at the envelope back first. And it usually costs little or nothing extra to print. One good technique is to use a strong headline on the *envelope flap*. Then, for example, you can include 5 or so benefits or 3 to 5 free bonuses in a bulleted format on the rest of the envelope back.

4. Use the inside of the envelope

A successful little-known technique used by one of my clients is to print on the *inside* of the envelope. This works especially well when you mail to your established customers. For example, you can present a listing of related products along with order information.

5. Put numbers in your teasers

Specificity sells. It is attention getting and is a credibility builder. Use the number, not the word. Examples:

"2 For the Price of 1"

"Saves You 4 Times as Much"

"1007 Insider Secrets of Millionaires"

6. Include a Q&A

A well-prepared question and answer segment provides a compelling format to answer any possible objections your prospect may have. The Q&A can be incorporated in a sales letter or brochure.

Tip: Make your last question a call to action. It can sound something like this question: "Okay. I'm impressed. How can I get the product?" Include here your 800 number and other order information.

7. Use testimonials

Perhaps the strongest credibility builder you could include in a sales letter are testimonials. There is something special, almost magical, in the honest thoughts and feelings of enthusiastic customers.

Always use full name, not initials, and the city and state or country. Of course, be sure to gain written permission from your customer to use the testimonial.

8. Include benefits on your order card

Since getting an order is the purpose of a sales letter, your order card is the most important element. Yet, most order cards are incredibly boring and ugly. Plus, they are often confusing.

By preparing the order card before the sales letter, you are forced to carefully think through the offer. Include 3-5 of your most powerful benefits. Present your offer clearly.

Remember, some people will read the order card first, before the sales letter. That's why it must be strong enough to close the sale all by itself.

9. Replace "I" and "my"

You'd be surprised how the words "I" and "my" creep into your copy. Eliminate all these you possibly can and replace them with these words: "you" and "your." This is perhaps the easiest way to improve any piece of advertising copy.

10. Read copy out loud

Before finalizing any copy, read it out loud. Or even more effective, ask a friend or family member to read it to you. All the rough spots or confusing sections will suddenly pop right out and you can eliminate them.

11. Use long copy

Remember the old saying: "The more you tell, the more you sell." Your goal should be to make the letter long enough to tell a complete story using every benefit you can. But at the same time, eliminate any and all unnecessary words.

As to length, a boring letter of one page is too long. Yet, an exciting letter full of benefits of interest to the reader can be 4, 8, 12, 16, 32, even 56 pages! One of these days I plan to test a 100-page letter just for fun!

12. The key to sales

Presented in a powerful way, *benefits* are the key to a sales message.

The technique I use to develop benefits is to study the product. Then I write a single benefit on a 3 × 5 card from the prospect's point of view. I can shuffle the cards so I use the most powerful first and the rest in descending order. On most products I prepare at least 25 and sometimes 150 to 250. These benefits are the real sales hot buttons.

13. Include features

Elements such as the size, weight, color, texture, strength, finish and materials used should be included in your copy. Not only do prospects want this information, your credibility is enhanced when features are included. You sound authoritative, like you know what you are doing.

14. Use a Courier typeface

All my tests as well as those by other marketers show that in body copy *Courier* pulls better response than any other typeface. Why is that? Direct mail is a personal medium. Courier, more than other typefaces, produces a personal feeling of communication, from me to you.

15. Always use black ink

For body copy, always use black ink. Do not use other colors, such as blue, green, purple or red. Black ink produces the sharpest contrast with any other background color.

Tip: *A quick and easy way to lift sales by 10-20% without any copy changes is this. Insist that your printer achieves maximum ink coverage. It should be dark black. In most direct mail the ink coverage is far too light, a pale gray, therefore tough to read. Invest in a special magnifying glass your printer can help you obtain to check the coverage*

16. Use a "Johnson Box"

One good way to make a Courier headline stand out is with the use of a Johnson Box at the top of your letter. Here is what a Johnson Box looks like:

```
★ ★ ★ ★ ★ ★ ★ ★ ★ ★ ★ ★ ★ ★ ★ ★ ★ ★ ★ ★
★                                        ★
★        To Make Courier Headlines Stand Out,     ★
★                                        ★
★              Present Them Like This          ★
★                                        ★
★ ★ ★ ★ ★ ★ ★ ★ ★ ★ ★ ★ ★ ★ ★ ★ ★ ★ ★ ★
```

17. Use Times New Roman

The classic Times Roman is an effective headline typeface. Why? It's easy to read. I use it on many of my sales letters as the headline. It's also a good choice for teaser copy on the envelope.

Here is a Times Roman typeface

Tip: *Do not experiment with the many new typefaces which tend to call attention to themselves. Your goal is a reader's focus on a message that inspires action.*

18. Break ending sentences

Do not end a sentence with a period at the bottom of any page of a sales letter. Break the sentence. This encourages your prospect to turn the page and keep reading.

19. Use instructional phrases

At the bottom of each page of a sales letter certain phrases also encourage continued reading. The best ones I've found for odd-number pages are "over please" and on even-number pages "go to page 3, page 5, page 7," etc.

20. Always use a headline

At the top of your sales letter it's possible to use the same headline as the envelope teaser. However, I've found results are better using a different, though related, headline.

21. Eliminate the logo

Contrary to what is taught in universities and business schools, beginning a letter with a logo is a major mistake. Why?

A company logo is a "me" message. It doesn't provide any benefit to the reader. You must open by answering a question every prospect who reads your copy subconsciously is asking: "So what?"

Tip: There is a place for a logo. Use your beloved company logo at the bottom of the last page of your sales letter. Of course, you can use it at the bottom of the first page of a one-page letter.

22. Offer a money-back guarantee

Offering an unconditional guarantee will always increase sales no matter what product or service you market.

The longer the guarantee, the more effective it is. Here is the ultimate guarantee:

> "The product is offered with an unconditional lifetime guarantee. If for any reason you are dissatisfied, you may return the product and upon request receive a prompt and courteous refund of every cent you've paid."

Of course, a lifetime guarantee may not be practical for your product. In that case, the longer the guarantee the better the sales will be. And the fewer refunds will be requested. For example, 30 days works better than 14 days, 60 days is better than 30, 6 months is better than 60 days, one year is better than 6 months.

23. Include a P.S.

Next to the headline, a P.S. is the best read part of a letter. A good P.S. strategy is to briefly restate the main benefit and a summary of the offer.

Tip: A handwritten P.S. can sometimes dramatically improve results.

24. Use margin notes

A good way to gain more attention for important blocks of copy is by using handwritten notes in the margins. For example:

Huge savings!
Please note
Important benefit
Don't miss out
Free gift
Free bonus

Tip: *Do not overuse margin notes. One, and not more than two, per page is most effective. Make sure they are in the same handwriting as the signature.*

25. Use handwritten graphic symbols

In your letter, prices crossed out and new ones inserted, check marks, arrows, etc., are more effective when handwritten. Here are some examples.

Was $99. Now less than half price—$49

26. Always sign letter

Never send out a sales letter (or any piece of correspondence) without a live signature. While a written signature personalizes any communication, often it is omitted with computer produced correspondence. This is a huge mistake. Not only should you sign them, use as bold a signature as possible.

Tip: *The best ink color to use for signature, margin notes and arrows, etc., is* reflex blue. *When you mark up the letter and sign the original, use a felt tip pen.*

27. Offer free gifts

I have never prepared a sales letter that didn't significantly improve response when one or several free bonuses are offered. I've had increases in response to an offer improve by more than 5 times over the offer without the gift.

Tip: *The secret of successfully using free gifts is this. Offer only highly salable products that customers would be inclined to buy even if they weren't free. Don't use failed products.*

28. Offer reward for immediate response

Everyone procrastinates. Remember this. In direct marketing, delay is death!

To encourage an immediate buying decision, some examples of effective offer strategies include:

- ✓ 3 early bird gifts if you order within 5 days
- ✓ special offer ends on a specific cutoff date, after which regular price applies

✓ limited supply which will not ever be made again when inventory is exhausted

✓ special bonus for first 100 respondents

29. Personalize the order card

People love to see their name in print. If you are personalizing just one element of a mailing, the best one is the order card. It also makes it easier for the prospect to order, which will significantly increase response.

30. *Use the word Free*

The most powerful word in selling anything is the word free. Use it on the envelope and in the letter. Also, don't forget to employ it on the order card.

31. *Add a lift letter*

A lift letter is a separate letter or note that helps improve, or lift, response.

The most effective type I've found is from a customer who is absolutely thrilled with your product or service. Nothing can replace it.

> ***Tip:*** *Here is an effective way to print the lift letter. On the back, handwrite these words: "In case you are still undecided." On the front, reprint the letter in its original form.*
>
> *Contrary to what you often see in direct marketing, a lift letter should always be from someone other than the signer of the main letter.*

32. Include a fax and Internet reply options

You will increase response with a fax and Internet options.

33. Use live stamps

You will usually get a 10–15% lift in response by using actual stamps and a metered or printed indicia.

If you mail first class, use a standard first class stamp. If you mail third class, use a bulk rate stamp. The post office often handles stamped third class mail just like first class.

Secrets of Envelope "Teaser" Copy Which Can Double Your Response!

Definition of "teaser" copy: Words printed on the outside of an envelope intriguing the recipient enough to open the letter. There is no chance of a sale, of course, unless prospect first opens the envelope.

Is "teaser" copy on outer envelopes the best sales strategy? Or is it better to use a plain envelope which is personalized?

The debate rages on.

In spite of all the evidence to the contrary, many still believe better results can be obtained without the use of "teaser" copy, as e.g. a plain envelope with typewritten address and live stamp.

My experience is this. Both views can be right. Why?

When your "teaser" copy is weak, it can reduce the number of people who open the envelope. In such a case, you are better off without it.

But when you create a "teaser" that is effective, you can more than double the response over any other envelope strategy that I've seen. That's why I favor it.

Clearly, I'm not alone in being an advocate of "teaser" copy. 100% of the most successful mailings by direct marketers during the last 10 years all have "teaser" copy on the outer envelope. (Success in this context is defined here as being profitably mailed for at least 3 years.)

Due to their substantial costs, these sales letters are continuously mailed in the millions for only one reason. They are generating profits.

How to prepare "teasers"

As with the headline in an ad or on a sales letter, the key to effective "teaser" copy on an envelope is beautiful in its simplicity.

Here is how to do it. Write down all the benefits that a customer can possibly get from your product or service. Prepare each one in a headline style using no more than 17 words. Then choose: ***the strongest benefit!***

To both illustrate the idea and get your creative juices flowing, here are a number of envelope "teasers" that have made money for years in my own companies and for clients:

(1) **How to Make Yourself Judgment Proof**

Lawsuit explosion in the U.S. makes it mandatory to protect yourself from judgments caused by creditors, customers, patients, IRS employees or even an ex-spouse

Secrets of Envelope "Teaser" Copy 151

(2) An urgent message from the publisher—
To be opened and read immediately

(3) **What Will You Do When
Your Personal Assets Are Seized
to satisfy a Judgment
Against Your Corporation?**

Free Sample Form Enclosed Protects You

(4) # Why Pay Taxes?
**Turn your business into a wealth-building
Tax Shelter. It's 100% legal! (See Page 1
of the $24.95 book you will soon
receive FREE.)**

(5) **Little Known Secret to Earning Millions Revealed**

See details enclosed . . .

(6) **World renowned doctor says** . . .

**"You Can Prevent
and Cure Cancer
Simply by Eating
Two Natural Foods!"**

7 Time Nobel Award nominated
doctor, Dr. Johanna Budwig,
discovers natural cancer cure

See Inside
for Details . . .

(7) **The Secret of Being a Great Boss—Do Less and Accomplish More!**

(8) *What Makes a Consultant Successful?*

(9) What If You Were Certain a Fortune in Gold Were Hidden Right In Your Home?
Would you spend 2 years of part-time effort to find it? . . .

See Free Treasure Map inside

(10) NEW

Stop Writing Letters the Hard Way

Announcing The *Instant* Letter Writing System.

Save 87% Of Your Correspondence Time.

And You Write Better Letters!

Free sample sales letter enclosed . . . Open immediately

A fascinating case history

Here is a short story from which you can learn much.

One of my most successful and loyal readers and friend is Jerry Minchey, who resides in Hilton Head, South Carolina.

Recently I got this letter from Jerry:

> Dear Ted,
>
> . . . I am now a firm believer in "teaser" copy. I mailed 12,000 letters. I broke the mailing into six groups. I tested two different headlines in each of three different envelopes.
>
> *The "teaser" envelope beat both the fake next-day envelope and the personal envelope with a personal note inside by two to one.* I will be printing on the envelope flap on the next mailing to improve the response even more. I have included a copy of each envelope for you to see.
>
> Thanks for teaching me about using "teaser" copy and, of course, about the value of testing.

Here is how the three envelopes looked:

154   How to Turn Words into Money

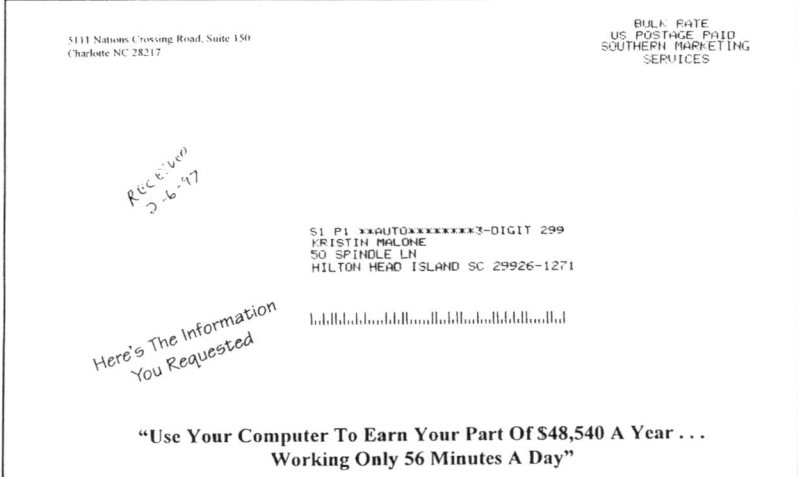

This envelope got twice the response

It's so important, I want to repeat this main point again.

The envelope with "teaser" copy, compared with the two others, was *twice* as effective!

And that's not all you can glean from Jerry's willingness to share his recent mailing experience.

Here are the results using exactly the same sales letter, but with two different headlines tested against one another.

Again, here is more from Jerry's letter.

> . . . the two headlines pulled *exactly* the same number of responses. One explanation may be that since I used a one million dollar bill clipped to the front of the letters, this may have been the "real" headline and that may have made the actual headline much less important in this case.
>
> Further analysis did prove interesting though. There is one question on our application that asks if they have the $7,000 to invest in the business.
>
> It seems people with money are interested in making more money and people without money are concerned about security or keeping what they have. Here are the results:
>
> Even though the actual number of responses was equal, 69% of the people who responded to the headline, "How to Use Your Computer to Earn Your Part of $48,540 a Year . . . Working Only 56 Minutes a Day" said they had the $7,000 to invest.
>
> Only 26% of the people responding to the headline, "Did You Swap Your Dream of Financial Independence For the 'Security' of a Job?" said they had the $7,000 to invest.

A good headline is *like a laser beam to your customers.*

The lessons to be derived here is that a good headline also *selects the right audience* for you.

Nearly 3 times (69%) as many *qualified buyers* of Jerry's business opportunity responded to the earning money appeal.

The *same number* of people responded to the alternate headline. But of these security-minded people, only 26% had the money to get involved in the business.

As you can see, the *type of people* that were attracted to the "money" headline were 300% better prospects for the offer.

The bottom line point is this. A powerful headline or "teaser" can do far more than increase response.

You can also: **Select the right audience!**

The kind of people who respond to any of your offers determines the final outcome. If you appeal to prospects who are *financially qualified*, as is done in this instance, clearly your chance of making the sale markedly increases. Therefore, for best results, when crafting headlines: **use appeals which benefit a highly qualified prospect.**

Jerry Minchey has an instinct for success. He sees the importance of valuable information he can put to use. He has attended virtually *every seminar* I've done in the last 12 years. He buys every tape set and studies every book I've ever released. Jerry is an uncommon man. And he gets outstanding results from his marketing efforts.

Unlike many unsuccessful entrepreneurs, Jerry invests money in the most important skill of all—*education*. Your knowledge is the single most valuable skill you have. Once possessed, it can never be taken away.

Contrary to popular belief, placing a high value on education is precisely the quality shared by the most successful new millionaires. Indeed, the wealthiest entrepreneurs of the world are lifelong

"Did You Swap Your Dream of Financial Independence For The 'Security' of A Job?"

(Now, how secure is your job?)

Tuesday 10:37 a.m.

Dear Friend,

As you can see, I have attached a one million dollar bill to this letter. Why have I done this? Actually, there are two reasons:

Number one, I have something very important to tell you and I need some way to <u>make sure</u> this letter gets your attention.

Number two, since what I have to tell you involves money, I thought using a one million dollar bill as a little financial eye-catcher would be especially appropriate.

Why am I so excited? The answer is simple. The enclosed brochure describes how you can . . .

<u>use your home computer to make up to $60 an hour working part-time or full-time</u>

How much extra money do you want?

What's so amazing is the extremely low investment required to get into this business and the very high profit margins made possible by this new technology.

But <u>technology can be a two-edged sword. It can create opportunity and it can take away your job</u>.

Let's face it. Technology is eliminating jobs at an alarming rate. Over **1,500 employees were fired today** or laid off and another 1,500 will lose their jobs tomorrow. Corporate downsizing is coming to <u>all</u> companies. It's not a matter of <u>if</u>, it's a matter <u>when</u>.

With all of the new technology, it just doesn't take as many workers, supervisors or managers to produce the same amount of goods or services. You can't blame the companies. If they don't downsize and stay competitive, they'll be forced out of business and you'll lose your job anyway.

Think about it. How good is your job? Do you enjoy it? Are you having fun? Are you making the kind of money you need to be financially secure? Does it look like things are going to get better in the future if you sit tight and do nothing?

Average people are going to do nothing and hope for the best. They're afraid to take a risk. That's the reason they'll go to their graves being <u>average</u>. The sad thing is, by doing nothing they're taking a tremendous risk.

Now you have the opportunity to live a lifestyle that's so superior to "average" you'll look back and say, "Why did I ever consider living the rest of my life with no security and with someone else totally in control, not only of the amount of my

Sales letter with headline A

"How To Use Your Computer To Earn Your Part Of $48,540 A Year . . . Working Only 56 Minutes A Day"

Don't bet your future on only one income stream . . . your job

Tuesday 10:37 a.m.

Dear Friend,

As you can see, I have attached a one million dollar bill to this letter. Why have I done this? Actually, there are two reasons:

Number one, I have something very important to tell you and I need some way to <u>make sure</u> this letter gets your attention.

Number two, since what I have to tell you involves money, I thought using a one million dollar bill as a little financial eye-catcher would be especially appropriate.

Why am I so excited? The answer is simple. The enclosed brochure describes how you can . . .

<u>use your home computer to make up to $60 an hour working part-time or full-time</u>

How much extra money do you want?

What's so amazing is the extremely low investment required to get into this business and the very high profit margins made possible by this new technology.

But <u>technology can be a two-edged sword. It can create opportunity and it can take away your job.</u>

Let's face it. Technology is eliminating jobs at an alarming rate. Over **1,500 employees were fired today** or laid off and another 1,500 will lose their jobs tomorrow. Corporate downsizing is coming to <u>all</u> companies. It's not a matter of <u>if</u>, it's a matter <u>when</u>.

With all of the new technology, it just doesn't take as many workers, supervisors or managers to produce the same amount of goods or services. You can't blame the companies. If they don't downsize and stay competitive, they'll be forced out of business and you'll lose your job anyway.

Think about it. How good is your job? Do you enjoy it? Are you having fun? Are you making the kind of money you need to be financially secure? Does it look like things are going to get better in the future if you sit tight and do nothing?

Average people are going to do nothing and hope for the best. They're afraid to take a risk. That's the reason they'll go to their graves being <u>average</u>. The sad thing is, by doing nothing they're taking a tremendous risk.

Now you have the opportunity to live a lifestyle that's so superior to "average" you'll look back and say, "Why did I ever consider living the rest of my life with no security and with someone else totally in control, not only of the amount of my

Sales letter with headline B

students. Self-made wealth builders tend to be very curious. And always interested in gaining more information to help become even more successful. "Know-it-all" types do not get far in life.

Tip: *To maximize your success, go to 8-12 seminars a year. Study the people who are masters in their field. Read a book every two weeks. Continue to learn and grow.*

The very first thing you should do when writing copy is to prepare headlines. Take time to do so, as nothing is more important in the marketing process.

I always write as many headlines as I possibly can. Some become "teasers." Those that I don't test are used as bullet points in ads and sales letters. Direct the focus of each headline on your best prospects. Use these headline strategies and watch your sales skyrocket!

Quick Summary

- The use of "teasers" and headlines can represent as much as 90% of your marketing results. Therefore, spend hours, days, and even weeks if necessary, creating them.
- Always use "teaser" copy on envelopes which offer a major benefit to a qualified prospect.
- Write lots of headlines, a many as you can. Use the headlines you don't choose to lead with as bullet points in your "bucket brigade" copy.
- Always use headlines on sales letters which offer a major benefit to a qualified prospect.
- Test more than one "teaser" and headline for best results.

38 Ways to Use FREE—The Most Powerful Word In Any Language

Free is the most powerful word in any language.

Over the years, Free has proven over and over again to be the strongest, most important word in marketing anything. Most marketers do use Free on occasion. But the use of the word Free is all too rare, even for experienced people. In fact, I've never seen a marketer overuse this most important selling word.

I recommend using Free at every opportunity. In ad headlines, on envelope "teaser" copy, in coupons, brochures, order cards, everywhere you can use copy to sell. No word gets more attention. Every time you use it correctly, sales will explode!

That's why it continues to baffle me when I review mail and notice that Free continues to be vastly underused. To me, it's a big mistake—analogous to owning a powerful tool such as a laser diamond cutter and keeping it in a closet while you labor at cutting diamonds by hand.

Since I haven't found any articles about this magic word anywhere else, I've devoted this chapter to the effective use of the word Free. Some examples I'll review will undoubtedly be familiar to you. If so, great. You are certainly on the right track.

But I'd be surprised if any reader has used even half of all the possibilities. Study this chapter carefully. I guarantee you'll be stimulated to use Free in ways you never before considered.

Here are many of the ways I use Free to market a variety of products and services.

1. Free Trial Request

If mail order advertisers had to select the most effective offer which has best stood the test of time, this would be their choice!

From the customer standpoint, who is being asked to buy from an unknown company in a distant city, a free trial relieves the fear of losing your money. Of course, when one can actually get the product and try it before paying for it, sales resistance is vastly lessened.

When selling on a free trial basis, you will more than double your response compared to a cash-up-front offer.

If your product is suited to a free trial offer, the length is an important decision.

1–14 days works well for many book and merchandise offers. 30 days or longer may be necessary for a more complicated product such as computer software. Or a home study course.

Under free trials, naturally more people will return products which are not kept for a variety of reasons. 10 to 25 percent is not unusual. But, if your sales more than double, it can be well worth the extra handling.

2. Free Sample

An incredibly powerful selling technique is to offer a free sample. This can be done in a mailing or in a retail store. When I was in the confectionery business, a free taste of fudge, chocolate or ice cream did wonders for sales.

In publishing books or information products that include forms, a sample form or agreement that the prospect can use becomes a powerful selling inducement. If your product can be sampled, I highly recommend allowing people to do so freely.

3. Free Gifts

Assuming your product has sales appeal, nothing you can do in a mailing can boost sales with more power than a free bonus gift. But the secret is it must be highly appealing. A good question to answer before you choose a free gift is: Would the prospect be willing to buy it if it weren't free?

Once you prepare a profitable offer that includes a free gift, it's always a good idea to continually test new free gifts to see if you can beat it.

4. Free Bonus For Prompt Response

An excellent sales closing technique is to offer a free gift to those who respond immediately. Here is one effective way to present the concept:

> *Free bonus for early birds*
>> If you respond within 10 days (or by November 30—a specific date is more effective) we will send you absolutely Free a valuable special report that will . . .

5. *Free Money*

I have used a copper penny, nickel, dime, a U.S. dollar bill and even failed currencies such as (worthless) Brazilian bank notes or old German marks attached to the top of a sales letter. Money always attracts attention in your mailings. An almost irresistible "teaser" on the envelope is something like:

> "Free money enclosed . . . please open at once!"

Your body copy can begin something like this:

"I am attaching a crisp new dollar bill to the top of this letter for two reasons:

1. To attract your attention.
2. To dramatize the amount of money you are about to earn in your relationship with Ted Nicholas."

6. Free Examination

An appealing way to entice a prospect to try your product is to let him/her examine it for a period of time. One effective way to present this concept is:

> "Examine this amazing air filter for 30 days at our risk, not yours. We won't cash your check or charge your credit card until 31 days after you've received it. If you are not pleased with the product, simply return it and we'll send back your uncashed check."

7. Free Name Reservation

This is a technique which encouraged many clients to reserve a name before incorporation in my formerly owned business, The Company Corporation.

If you can offer a free service in your business that both helps the customer while increasing their commitment to you, it can be an effective marketing tool.

8. News of 3 Free Gifts Inside

I use this teaser phrase on the outside of envelopes to encourage the receiver to open and read, which is 90% of the battle!

Of course, never use any copy that isn't absolutely true. It's both immoral and illegal. If you trick someone into opening an envelope and the inside contents do not meet the promise made on the envelope, prospects will stop reading your offer. Plus, you will turn people off from doing business with you at that point and probably in the future as well.

9. Send For Free Information

When you offer to send free information, also use these words: "Without obligation. No salesman will call." Prospects find these phrases very appealing. Many people are wary about having to deal with pushy salespeople.

10. Send for Free Booklet

Booklets pull inquiries if the copy is powerful and the benefits offered are appealing. Regardless of your business, valuable free information is a terrific inducement to contact you.

11. Buy One, Get One Free

The offer you create to sell your product is very important. And not well understood by most. Changing an offer can often be the most important thing you can do to improve response. Just restating an offer can double or triple response. For example, "buy one, get one free" pulls better than "50% off."

Some years ago the Mary Carter Paint Company built a huge international business on this offer:

"Buy one can of paint—get one free"

12. Free Initial Consultation

This is an outstanding offer, particularly for professional services, such as legal, medical, accounting, massage, fitness, etc. It's important for any personal service to answer the question in the mind of everyone, "Am I really going to like the dentist (or other professional)?"

I highly recommend this approach to any professional seeking to build a practice because it lets prospects try you before they buy you.

13. Free Test Enclosed

Can be a compelling involvement device. I've created a test for a health book offer. The offer reads:

"Free prostate test for men over 40 enclosed"

Do you have or can you create an appealing test in your business? If so, lots of people may take it and subsequently do business with you.

14. Free Door Prize

For many offers, especially in retailing or seminars, this has an enormous appeal.

A retail store can offer door prizes at special sales. If you are conducting free or preview seminars, many more people will come if there is a door prize offered.

15. Free Bonus Points

A terrific sales enhancer for clubs or frequent customer programs. You're undoubtedly familiar with frequent flyer programs offered by airlines and their wide appeal. You can create your own version for your business.

16. Free Contest

A contest can be a highly captivating addition to many offers. Contests which involve numbers or facts about a variety of subjects as well as crossword puzzles are part of an enormous number of possibilities. It's better when the contest relates directly or indirectly to your type of business.

17. First Month's Rent Free

Any time you give away free rent, the sales power of real estate, automobile and other rental offers are obviously enhanced.

Large transactions, such as a full floor in an office building, are often concluded when longer periods of time "sweeten" the offer, such as "6 months" or "one year free."

If you are negotiating a lease yourself for office space or a new apartment, it's always good strategy to ask whether you can have some free rent as part of the deal.

18. Free Lesson

If you are a teacher of subjects such as music, tennis, or French, you'll get a lot more takers to try your service by offering a free lesson. Prospects feel a lot more comfortable without having to make a long commitment up front.

19. Free Vacation

If you have resort properties to sell, offering prospects the chance to stay free may entice people to try out the property. If they like it, you will have buyers.

20. Free Day As Our Guest

Let's say you have just opened your own bed and breakfast. A great offer is:

"Come for the weekend and get one day absolutely free"

21. Free Refills

If you operate a restaurant or bar, you'll sell a lot more beverages if people can get free refills during certain times. You can create a deluxe happy hour program with great appeal.

22. Free Car Wash

Gasoline and service stations can sell a lot more fuel and other products if they offer free car washes along with any purchase over a certain amount, i.e. $20.

23. Free Oil Change

A service station or mechanic that offers a profitable engine tune-up program as a bonus can create more customers when they get a free oil change.

*Products that have proven to be
outstanding Free Bonuses include . . .*

24. Free Special Report

Regardless of what the main product or service is that you offer, special reports which are relevant and wanted by your prospect will increase sales. Providing the report is perceived to provide lots of valuable information, you can offer your product within the report and often get a high response.

25. Free Book

All sorts of books make appealing free gifts. You can offer a best-selling well-known book or simply almost any book that is relevant to your prospect. Dictionaries also make fine bonus items, as nearly everyone values them.

26. *Free Tape*

A video or audio cassette of high quality is the perfect bonus for many offers.

If you offer a product or service which is enhanced by color and visuals, such as jewelry or Caribbean property, by all means use video cassettes. After production costs, in quantity they can be very economical, i.e. $2-$6.

27. Free Software

A computer disk, or a CD Rom, can enhance many offers. When your customers love the free one, you can offer an advanced version of your product and have many takers.

28. Free Newsletter

A free newsletter is perhaps the biggest sleeper and least known powerhouse among all bonus gifts. A well-written newsletter containing valuable information also makes an excellent continuing communication tool with prospects and customers.

The best part of all is that newsletters can be habit forming. Your customers will look forward to getting it and hearing from you on a regular basis.

29. Free Calculators

Even though most people have at least one calculator, everyone seems to like getting new ones. A free one has a surprisingly strong impact on sales for nearly every offer.

30. Free Luxury Car

No, I'm not joking! If you sell high priced products such as the $5,000,000 mansions as does one of my readers, or Lear jets by another, you can enhance a sale by offering a Free Mercedes, Jaguar or Porche!

One of my most successful promotions of the mailing list in a publishing offer was a "Free Rolls Royce delivered to your office just for testing the hottest mailing list in America"! But it was not a full-size car. The ad described a beautiful 1/20th *replica* of the car! The car cost $100 wholesale. But it was well worth it to us because each client was so valuable. It made a very appealing gift highly treasured by its recipients; so much good will was created.

31. Free Map

A detailed map or book of maps can enhance many offers. Obviously if your business is travel related, a map is an ideal gift.

32. Free Swiss Army Knife

A pocket knife engraved with the name of the buyer profitably increased the sales of one client who sells $2,000 software products by over 30%.

33. Free Gold Coin

A free gold or silver coin is being successfully used by various marketers, including newsletter and book publishers and coin sellers, as an inducement to "buy now."

34. Free Beer Mug

A beer mug designed with an authentic German design has markedly enhanced a high priced software offer. Surprisingly, the offer is mailed to executives, yuppies and computer buffs who may not be thought of as enthusiastic beer drinkers.

35. Free T-Shirt

Many offers are enhanced by offering a free gift T-shirt. For some reason no matter how many T-shirts people have, they continue to have wide appeal.

36. Free Hat

A hat, such as a baseball style visor cap with a logo or attractive decoration, makes an appealing bonus gift.

37. Children Are Free

When you make an offer for an event and allow someone such as a spouse or child to attend at no cost, you can substantially increase sales.

38. Bring One Guest Free

You can enhance attendance at any event or seminar by offering to allow the paying participant to bring any guest they wish.

Good sources for many free gifts are companies which sell premiums and advertising specialties, as well as publishers. Look in your Yellow Pages as a place to start. You can also attend gift and premium trade shows for items discussed here. Plus, you may get new ideas.

Don't you enjoy free gifts? I'll bet you do! I do too! Almost everyone does.

You will get a greater response to your ads, mailings and sales calls when you enhance offers with the most powerful word in any language. Free.

Before you plan any marketing campaign, always ask yourself this question. "In what ways can I use the biggest word friend I've got—the magic word 'Free'?" Watch your sales grow.

How to Launch a Hot New Product

Regardless of what business you are in, to be successful as an entrepreneur you need to be proficient at launching new products and services.

In this issue, I will reveal the secrets behind what looks like the most successful product launch I've ever had. And I've been involved with many of them.

This information provides an asset which, in the right hands, is worth many millions of dollars! I'll help you put together a *template* for your future product launches.

Plus, you'll have more fun in your business life. Launching a new product can be almost as exciting as the birth of a child!

The first step in a product launch is to establish a *goal*. My goal in creating my most recent product: to bring my work in marketing to more people in every free market country throughout the world. This will be done through information products, including books, tapes and seminars.

The "lead" product is my book MAGIC WORDS THAT BRING YOU RICHES. The book contains the best of the discoveries I've made plus marketing principles I've developed. I also share the key ways the reader's personal life can be vastly improved.

The first thing I did after deciding to create a product based on the awesome power of words in every language was **write an ad!**

Preparing an advertisement was a powerful step. Why? It forced me to think through and dramatize the product's benefits from the prospect's point of view. This finding the benefits process also enabled me to create a far more saleable product. Too many products are produced first, before a marketing plan is conceived. A major mistake.

I then sent the ad to some friends. Nearly all wanted to order the product.

The next thing I did right after conceiving the product idea was to think through the "back end." Most marketers make the mistake of not planning follow-up products ("back-end" products) when launching a new product.

Don't you make this common mistake. No matter how hot, you cannot live on any single product. You must have follow-up products and services.

Tip: Always plan at least one follow-up product before you launch your new product.

What is the "back end" for the Magic Word Book?

1. A $500 audio tape set

2. Catalog products

3. Seminars

4. New clients for marketing and copy

Print advertising strategy

Space ads, both one-step (sales off the page) and two-step (inquiry ads followed up with direct mail).

Expansion

After successful tests were completed in the U.S., licensees were recruited in every free market country in the world. Licensees were appointed in the United Kingdom, Australia, Germany, France and Switzerland. The book as well as all advertising materials were translated verbatim in non-English speaking countries. Licensees pay me a 10% royalty on sales. In return, they receive a license to get rich with proven products and tested ad copy.

Licensing also provides a great benefit for me. It saves time while simplifying international expansion and avoids the formidable task of becoming an expert in all of the local nuances, such as mailing tests, print media, etc. in every country.

Once a mailing list of buyers (a new database) of "Magic Words" was created in each of the countries, mailings for tapes and seminars will be made.

Early results

Two test one-step space ads using different appeals were run. One pulled a profitable 2 times ad cost, the other an amazing 11 times ad cost! Test ads were run in a Salt Lake City newspaper during August. Additional tests were run in October in *USA Today* and in an *Airline Magazine*.

Two-step ads were run in weekly newspapers. The lead costs came in at a cost 67¢ to $3.74 each. A follow-up series of 10 follow-up letters were sent with satisfactory conversions. Additional two-step ads were run in the September and October. Media include *Wall Street Journal*, various *airline magazines*, *Christian Science Monitor*, and *Capper's*.

Sales projections

Sales of 100,000 books in the U.S. from space ads were projected during the first year. Follow-up tapes were projected at 10,000 units.

Seminar seats from the new program were projected at 2,000. Acceptable and qualified new clients were projected and limited to a total of 10.

A T.V. Infomercial

We have also filmed a 30-minute television commercial program (infomercial) entitled, surprise, surprise, "Magic Words That Bring You Riches." The offer includes the book as well as some audio and video tapes. This package of products will be tested at 3 prices—$89.97, $119.97 and $149.97.

While T.V. can generate volume sales rapidly, few infomercials go beyond the test stage. Only 1 out of 15 infomercials make money. Reason? Audience is very general. You cannot isolate and target audiences as well as you can in space ads and direct mail. Experience has proven specialized products have a far higher chance of success with a highly targeted audience, rather than a mass market.

> ***Tip:*** *If you have a product or service where the main prospects are part of a large but specialized audience, if the budget allows you might want to test T.V. among the media you select. However, since the biggest cost in all advertising is waste circulation, the odds against T.V. working are far higher than with more traditional direct response*

Magic Words That Bring You Riches
FREE report is yours for the asking

The single most important activity of your life is your ability to communicate. Unlimited success and wealth is as simple as using the right words which work as if by magic!

Suppose Ted Nicholas, one of the highest paid speakers and writers in the world, revealed to you the exact words that have been proven to work best in virtually every situation? Ted has prepared a Free special report, "MAGIC WORDS THAT BRING YOU RICHES."

Ted is a marketing genius. His books include "How To Form Your Own Corporation Without A Lawyer For Under $75"; "The Golden Mailbox— How to Get Rich Direct Marketing Your Product"; and "MAGIC WORDS THAT GET YOU EVERYTHING YOU WANT IN LIFE." He is perhaps the highest paid writer and speaker per *word* in the world. He earns as much as $500,000 from a single 1,000 word ad. Ted has invested over $100,000,000 in tests to find exactly the right words. Once revealed they will work for you, too. Certain words are extremely powerful. For example:

- Saying 2 magic words will always get you the best table in any restaurant in the world.
- 7 magic words will bring you job offers even during tough economic times.
- 9 magic words provide unlimited money for your business ventures.
- Get advertising in national magazines free with 17 magic words.
- Cut costs of travel by 50% or more with 6 magic words.
- Discover exact words that can earn you millions from your own advertisements or letters.
- Obtain the exclusive rights to bestselling products for as little as $250 with 23 magic words.
- These 27 magic words will empower you to sell anything to anyone.

To receive the special report, "MAGIC WORDS THAT BRING YOU RICHES," absolutely FREE, call toll-free, 24 hours a day: 1-800-730-7777.

Ask for the "Free Magic Word Report." Leave your name and mailing address and it will be rushed to you.

© 1995 Nicholas Direct, Inc.

Two-step inquiry ad

"Magic Words That Bring You Riches"

"At age 37 I found myself dead broke and $250,000 in debt. No matter how hard or how many hours I worked, I couldn't seem to get ahead. I had a wife and 4 children at home."

"Then I made a discovery. I became debt free in less than 6 months with over $100,000 in my bank account! I then went on to make millions. As much as $3,500,000 in a single year! And the best part of all? Instead of being tough to do, once you know how, it's surprisingly easy! And I'm convinced, once shown the way, you, too, can duplicate this success. The secret?"

"Learning the right words which work in every situation as if by magic. And I'll reveal every magic word, the precise word, to use," says best-selling author, Ted Nicholas!

The single most important activity of your life is your ability to communicate. The whole key to incredible success and wealth is contained within the words we use.

Words have incredible power. Words can move us to march for peace. Or go to war. Or laugh. Or cry. Or buy!

You are only a headline away from a fortune! Unlimited success and wealth can be yours. Imagine what it would be like to be equipped with exactly the right words to use in ads, negotiations, sales letters and personal encounters. You'll feel almost as though you have an unfair advantage over everyone with whom you come into contact!

Certain Words Work Like Magic!

Ted Nicholas, one of the highest paid writers and speakers in the world, will reveal to you the exact words that have proven to work best in virtually every situation.

Ted has prepared a new book containing all his word secrets. Its title is, *"MAGIC WORDS THAT BRING YOU RICHES"*. (This new book is not available in any bookstore.)

Ted is a marketing genius. His books include the best-seller with over 1 million copies in print, HOW TO FORM YOUR OWN CORPORATION WITHOUT A LAWYER FOR UNDER $75. Others include: THE GOLDEN MAILBOX – HOW TO GET RICH DIRECT MARKETING YOUR PRODUCT and HOW TO PUBLISH A BOOK AND SELL A MILLION COPIES.

Ted Nicholas is perhaps the highest paid writer and speaker per word in the world. He has earned as much as $1,000,000 writing just 1,000 words of ad copy, a single ad, promoting products sold in magazine ads or sales letters both for himself and select clients.

Ted's success with words is not based on theory. He has invested over $100,000,000 of his own money in tests to find the exact combination of words that work best in advertising.

Ted's new book shows you how to get very rich in marketing yourself or products. But it's much more. He also discovered and has refined the art of successfully using words in numerous personal and business situations we all face every day.

Examples of What You'll Learn:

- Saying 2 magic words will always get you the best table in any restaurant in the world. *Page 11*
- 7 magic words will bring you job offers even during tough economic times. *Page 19*
- 9 magic words provide unlimited money for your business ventures. *Page 25*
- Get advertising in national magazines free with 17 magic words. *Page 114*
- Cut costs of travel by 50% or more with 6 magic words. *Page 17*
- Discover exact words that can earn you millions from your own advertisements or letters. *Page 127*
- Obtain the exclusive rights to best-selling products for as little as $250 with 23 magic words. *Page 77*
- These 27 magic words will empower you to sell anything to anyone. *Page 119*
- Often get first class or business class seats on an airplane, even though you have coach tickets. *Page 13*
- Approach an attractive woman or man and immediately interest them in you. *Page 24*
- Rent a Mercedes automobile for the price of a Ford anywhere. *Page 35*
- Find a great gourmet cook to prepare low cost meals for you. *Page 39*
- Slash the cost of lodging in first class hotels by 50% or more. *Page 21*
- Get invited to speak before any group you choose and enhance your business career. *Page 43*
- Receive free expert consulting help for your business. *Page 47*
- Buy beautiful jewelry, including gold rings and watches at below wholesale. *Page 51*
- Earn over $100,000 in the most profitable business in the world, and start it for under $600. *Page 55*
- Find world famous people to speak before your group, free. *Page 59*
- Attract the world's best employees using powerful help wanted ads. *Page 63*
- Get capable people to work for you for free. *Page 67*
- Get free advertising by becoming a celebrity; first locally, then nationally. *Page 73*
- Reduce or eliminate legal fees in both your business and personal life. *Page 81*
- Buy valuable antiques at huge discounts. *Page 85*
- Get valuable financial interests in other people's companies without investing one red cent. *Page 89*
- Earn from $100,000 to $250,000 a year and more as a consultant by making an offer almost no one can turn down. *Page 93*

A special section reveals the secrets behind Ted's successful print ads and mailings. These will include the powerful strategy behind these magic words, which can earn you $500,000 to $1,000,000 or more per year on your products and services!

What People Say About Ted Nicholas

"I'm from a working class family and was working as a struggling private investigator. Then you taught me the power of magic words. In the past 12 months I earned $1,700,000!"
–Mike Enlow

"Thank you for the guidance in writing several best-sellers, including Crisis Investing."
– Doug Casey

"In 30 days your techniques earned me $15,000."
–Francois Blot

"Your magic words helped me earn over $1,000,000 last year!"
–Cindy Cashman

"Top secret information worth millions of dollars in the right hands."
–Blade Thomas

"Your willingness to share failures as well as achievements has helped me avoid repeating these errors."
–Jack Pugsley

"Your work delivers all valuable 'meat'; no fluff."
–Lee Milteer

"No human being alive knows more about making magazine advertising pay off."
–Gary Halbert

Sworn Statement

"I was Ted Nicholas' bookkeeper for 7 years and helped prepare his tax returns. To the best of my knowledge, everything he has stated in this message is absolutely true and accurate."
–Gail Waterman

Special Offer

A limited edition of this remarkable book has been printed and is available by mail. You are now able to reserve a copy while supplies last at a special price if you order now. To avoid disappointment, don't delay.

Free Bonus

If you respond within 14 days, you will be sent a beautiful rendition of what many call Ted's most valuable secret and to which he attributes 90% of his success. Done in calligraphy and suitable for framing, people have happily paid as much as $1,500 to learn it. Act now, and it's yours free to keep absolutely free.

For fastest service, call at once 1-800-730-7777. Credit card orders can be faxed to 1-813-596-6900. Or mail coupon now.

Money Back Guarantee

After you receive the book and examine it for a full 3 months, if for any reason you are not completely happy, return it undamaged for a prompt and courteous refund.

☐ **Yes.** Please rush a copy of MAGIC WORDS THAT BRING YOU RICHES by Ted Nicholas at $19.97 plus $4 shipping & handling. I understand that if for any reason I am not delighted with the book, anytime within 90 days, I may return it undamaged for a prompt and courteous refund. And I may keep my free bonus regardless.

☐ Enclosed is my check.
☐ Please charge my:
  ☐ Visa ☐ MC ☐ AmEx

Card Number _____ Expiration Date _____

Signature _____

Name _____

Address _____

City/State/Zip _____

Daytime Phone _____
(if we have a question on your order)

Nicholas Direct, Inc., 1511 Gulf Blvd., Dept. #
P. O. Box 877, Indian Rocks Beach, FL 34635
© Copyright 1995 Nicholas Direct, Inc.

"Magic Words" Space Ad—Version A

"It Amazed My Friend... I Said Two Simple Words. And We Were Escorted to the Finest Table in the Restaurant!"

And you'll never guess what they are! Yes, knowing the right words to say will get you everything you want in life

I'll never forget the look on her face. Pure joy!

You've surely had this experience. You make dinner reservations. You are taken to your table. Inevitably it's in a poor location. Usually by the kitchen where it's noisy. Or by the drafty front door. Oddly enough this often happens, even when the restaurant is not busy. It used to happen to me all the time. Until...

I learned the secret. Now I always get the very best table, wherever I go.

Certain Words Are Magic

One day while on vacation, it hit me like a bolt of lightning! Not only special treatment in restaurants, but all the good fortune I enjoy happens for just one reason. Because of words. Simple ones.

My name is Ted Nicholas. As a writer and speaker, I've been fascinated with words and phrases all my life. I've been refining these words for years. I've taught friends to say them. The same remarkable results happen to them.

No one is misled. Every word is truthful. Best of all, these words work for anyone.

Knowing the right words to say are responsible for my earning millions. As much as $3,500,000 in a single year. Getting 13 best-selling books published. Owning two, million dollar homes. Driving a new Mercedes convertible. And traveling throughout the world.

Think of it. I'm a college dropout. I began my career with no writing or speaking skills. No money. No contacts. No wealth, friends or relatives. No special privileges of any kind. And remarkable things have happened. All because of the power of these words.

Magic Words Will Change Your Life

I've decided to share these secrets for the very first time in my new book. I'll give you every word And to whom. In all types of situations which you face daily. You will then be in a position to enhance your life beyond what you've ever imagined. My book is called MAGIC WORDS THAT BRING YOU RICHES.

I know the book title sounds almost too good to be true. A little skeptical? I would be too if I were you. But don't worry. The "words" will work for you. You will be more successful at everything you do. And you'll enjoy it far more, too! Or the book won't cost you a dime! I'll reveal the secrets of how to:

- Always get the best table in any restaurant in the world. (And you won't have to spend one cent in tips to get it!) (page 11)
- Often get first class or business class seats on an airplane, even though you have coach tickets. (page 13)
- Have employers clamoring to call you with job offers, even during tough economic times. (This powerful technique never before in print anywhere will boggle your mind and get you the job you really want!) (page 19)
- Attract all the money you need for any business venture. (page 25)
- Approach an attractive woman or man and immediately interest them in you. (page 24)
- Rent a Mercedes automobile for the price of a Ford anywhere. (page 35)
- Find a great gourmet cook to prepare low cost meals for you. (page 39)
- Slash the cost of lodging in first class hotels by 50% or more. (page 21)
- Get invited to speak before any group you choose and enhance your career. (page 43)
- Receive free expert consulting help for your business. (page 38)
- Buy beautiful jewelry, including gold rings and watches at below wholesale. (page 40)
- Earn over $100,000 in the most profitable business in the world, and start it for under $600. (page 42)
- Find world famous people to speak before your group, free. (page 59)
- Attract the world's best employees using can't miss ads. (page 63)
- Get capable people to work for you for free. (page 67)
- Get free advertising by becoming a celebrity first locally, then nationally. (page 56)
- Obtain the U.S. rights to market best selling products from around the world for as little as $250. (page 77)
- Reduce or eliminate legal fees in both your business and personal life. (page 62)
- Buy valuable antiques at huge discounts. (Page 85)
- Get valuable, financial interests in other people's companies without investing one red cent. (page 89)
- Earn from $100,000 to $250,000 a year and more as a consultant by making an offer almost no one can turn down. (page 93)

A special section of my latest successful print ads and mailings is included that reveals powerful strategies which can earn you $500,000 or more on your products!

Sworn Statements

"I was Ted Nicholas' bookkeeper for 7 years and helped prepare his tax returns. To the best of my knowledge, everything he has stated in this message is absolutely true and accurate."
Gail Waterman

"I've known Ted Nicholas for some time now. He is a charming man and highly successful writer and speaker. However, when he told me of his new book I was more than skeptical that these ideas would work this side of the Atlantic. He gave me three ideas to try out for myself.
1. Within 4 weeks I found the best personal assistant I've ever employed.
2. I got free business advice that has already been worth over £20,000 to my company.
3. I now ALWAYS get the very best service at every restaurant I visit.
Now the book is ready I can't wait to work my way through his other great ideas!"
Mike Chantry
Hilite Ltd.
London, England

Special Offer

A limited edition of this remarkable book is ready. You are now able to reserve a copy while supplies last at a special price if you order now. To avoid disappointment, call immediately (800) 730-7777. Fax to (813) 596-6900 or complete the coupon below.

Money Back Guarantee

After you receive the book and examine it for 60 days, if for any reason you are not completely happy, return it undamaged for a prompt and courteous refund.

☐ Yes. Please rush a copy of MAGIC WORDS THAT BRING YOU RICHES, by Ted Nicholas at $19.97 plus $4 shipping & handling. I understand that if for any reason I am not delighted with the book, I may return it undamaged for a prompt and courteous refund.

☐ Enclosed is my check
☐ Please charge my:
  ☐ Visa ☐ MC ☐ AmEx

Card Number _____ Expires _____
Signature _____
Name _____
Address _____
City/State/Zip _____
Daytime Phone (if we have a question on your order) _____

Nicholas Direct, Inc.
Dept. 00-0
P.O. Box 877
Indian Rocks Beach, FL 34635
© 1995 Nicholas Direct, Inc.

"Magic Words" Space Ad—Version B

(The Advanced Home Study Course)

"Magic Words That Bring You Riches"

Dear Friend,

To increase your mastery of magic words, you simply must get the advanced Home Study Course. Every exciting moment was recorded at a recent Ted Nicholas "Magic Words" Seminar held in London. Why?

The seminar title was MILLION DOLLAR SALES SECRETS. But its real theme is "Magic Words That Bring You Riches." Every powerful word was captured on tape. It's been reproduced and is now available as an advanced home study course especially for owners of Ted's book, MAGIC WORDS THAT BRING YOU RICHES. An enormous amount of valuable information was presented that was <u>not</u> in the book.

You'll be able to discover more secrets about harnessing the power of magic words. Listen and learn while at home, exercising or in your car.

<u>**Gain what will seem like unfair advantage!**</u>

Hearing the tapes is like picking Ted Nicholas' brain! You will gain access to the very <u>latest new techniques</u> and strategies Ted is currently using to market millions of dollars worth of products throughout the world. Plus, Ted is one of America's best public speakers. This inside information will give you an all <u>important edge</u> possessed by few others. Discover what marketing techniques work best in the U.S. and also in England, Germany, France, Switzerland, Australia, and Asia.

The best part of all is people in several non-U.S. countries are <u>2 to 4</u> times <u>as responsive</u> as in the U.S.! Selling your product or service outside the U.S. is so easy! It's just like having an unfair advantage! You will learn why.

It used to be the U.S. represented 2/3 of the world market. No longer. Now it's just 1/3. Two-thirds of all goods sold today are outside the U.S.

Every successful entrepreneur wants to know how to sell to this huge universe. Plus, you will have a more international perspective, which will <u>increase your success</u> odds for everything you do in the U.S.

<u>**You can become very rich with a great way to do business!**</u>

Ted has earned as much as $3,500,000 in a single year. He'll

(please turn to page 2

Follow-up letter sent to inquiries

show you how you can start with little or no capital. Ted started with a $90 classified ad and sold $500,000,000 worth of products and services. Earn $12,404 per month in additional income--488% profit in a single month.

Sell your product worldwide from your easy chair as easily as you now sell locally. This is just one of many benefits you'll get from this amazing seminar. Hear every word presented live and unedited to a group of British entrepreneurs. The question and answer sessions are priceless!

Plus, you may be able to get Ted Nicholas, perhaps today's most successful international direct marketer, to be your own personal mentor and coach! More about that in a moment.

On the home study course you'll discover:

- 6 easy ways to find hot new product opportunities. You can have a million dollar new product idea every half hour!
- Put Ted's 5 secret principles to work in your life which assure success and make failure impossible!
- Grab attention in your ads by learning the latest secrets of writing powerful headlines.
- What opportunities found in the U.K. can easily be duplicated in the U.S. (and vice versa) with almost guaranteed profits.
- 7 compelling sub headlines (the actual words) that will make your ads more powerful.
- 5 magic phrases, word for word, to place on your envelopes that almost guarantee your sales letter will be opened.
- How to raise all the money you need, yet limit your financial risk. (Remember, Ted began with a $90 ad, and so can you).
- Determine which new products have the highest probability of success.
- Acquire the rights to a hot existing product with a track record of success for as little as $250 (if you don't already have a product of your own) just by saying the right words.
- Create direct mail letters and space ads with the highest probability of success.
- Select the right media in which to advertise among magazines, newspapers, catalogs, radio, T.V., card decks, or the hottest new media---electronic bulletin boards!
- Unleash the power of today's best low-cost/no-cost marketing strategies.
- Secrets of pricing products for maximum profit.
- Prepare the ideal sales letter for your product that is almost irresistible.
- Learn the art of testing---the real key to marketing success.
- Become exposed to the 27 most effective words in your ads to sell your product. (This recently revised list, proven by tests, works as though by magic and will earn you all the money you really want!)

(please go to page 3)

- Get up to an <u>80%</u> <u>discount</u> when you purchase magazine and newspaper ads by knowing the magic negotiating words-—exactly what to say! (This session alone could be worth hundreds of thousands, even millions, of dollars to you.)
- <u>Legally</u> <u>protect</u> your <u>products</u>, <u>ads</u> and <u>sales</u> <u>letters</u> at no cost. Prevent others from cashing in on your success.
- Get <u>free</u> <u>publicity</u> in newspapers and on radio and T.V.
- Determine the <u>most</u> <u>ideal</u> <u>business</u> in the world for you.
- Run <u>small</u> <u>classified</u> <u>ads</u> and build a mail order business, perhaps the <u>ideal</u> <u>retirement</u> <u>activity</u>.

Comments from seminar attendees from around the world

"Have attended many seminars, including those at the university gaining my Economics degree. None has taught me as much as I have learned from you. It's simply the best-- the experience of a lifetime."

C. Neophytou
London, England

"Although I've been in marketing for over 30 years, I've learned more in these three days than I believed possible. Thank you for the opportunity."

Gil Evans
Palm Harbor, Florida

"Your Marketing information on tape is worth more than 10 times its cost. In 30 days your techniques earned me $15,000.00."

Francois Blot
Chantilly, France

"There's probably no human alive who knows more about how to make magazine advertising pay off than Ted Nicholas. For the record, Ted Nicholas has my absolute highest recommendation! Ted you have just given the most valuable seminar I ever attended."

Gary Halbert
Key West, Florida

"You really put your money where your mouth is. With your sincere interest in really helping your seminar attendees."

Norman Rentrop
Bonn, West Germany

(please turn to page 4)

"Ted: Not only was your seminar fantastic for newcomers, it was equally valuable to those who are already established. Your expertise has shown me how we can increase sales on our existing products, and create new products and take them to new heights as well. Thanks for sharing your life experiences with us. It's the greatest form of education I know. Thanks again."

Deanna Polk
Hagerstown, Maryland

"Your home study course reveals the most valuable information for entrepreneurs in the world today! Top Secret--worth millions of dollars in the right hands."

Blade Thomas
Malibu, California

"Ted Nicholas has made fortunes for himself and others with his direct marketing knowledge. Treat any advice you get from this man as nuggets of the purest direct marketing gold, for that's what he's giving you."

Gary Bencivenga
Garden City, New York

"I'm a lawyer by education. Ted Nicholas inspired me to get into my own business. His home study course helped me write the first full-page ad I've ever attempted. Best marketing ideas I've heard..."

Mark Warda
Clearwater, Florida

Ted Nicholas makes unprecedented offer -- but you must qualify

There are two parts to this Ted Nicholas Super Deluxe Home Study Program.

1. <u>MILLION DOLLAR SALES SECRETS, *Magic Words That Bring You Riches* -- The Home Study Course</u>

    You will receive the complete home study course professionally recorded in London. You will also receive a workbook which contains all the valuable handout materials, sample ads, sale letters -- everything. As you drive your car, relax at home, walk or exercise, you'll receive a wealth of usable information.

2. <u>Personal Consultation with Ted</u>

    Suppose you could actually get Ted Nicholas to personally

(please go to page 5)

provide consultation on copy for your product? Do you think the odds of success would increase in your favor?

You bet they would! That's exactly why clients wait in line to pay Ted $15,000 plus 5% of sales to write copy for a sales letter or space ad. Ted also accepts 25% of the stock in the client's company in lieu of fees in some cases. Clients pay a minimum of $3,850 for a 1/2 day consultation.

If you have an acceptable product or service, you will receive at your request a personal written consultation by Ted Nicholas. This includes a critique along with specific suggestions. If needed, you will be given a new headline and letter opening written by Ted himself! You have an entire year to request this service after your application is accepted.

Of course, due to the personal nature of this arrangement, Ted must reserve the right to turn down an application. For any reason whatsoever. For example, if you are a marketer of a product or service of an "adult" product or one that could cause bodily harm, or is sold mainly via multi-level programs, please do not apply. (Of course, this is not to suggest there is anything at all negative about such products. For a variety of reasons, Ted simply doesn't get involved in promotions of this kind.)

If you were paying the usual fees individually for the critique and this Super Deluxe Home Study Program, your investment would be significant. At least $15,000. (Many people have paid $7,500 per person plus travel expenses to attend the Ted Nicholas Seminar.) And frankly, it would be worth every penny.

But, if your enclosed application is accepted, your investment will not be $15,000. Or $10,000. Or even $2,500.

Your total investment, including the Home Study Course and the optional critique is only $477. That's not a misprint. But you must act now!

Limited availability

This offer is strictly subject to acceptance and may be withdrawn at any time. You must qualify. It is not for everyone. If your application is not accepted for any reason, it will be returned along with your payment. Of course, your credit card will not be charged in such a case.

Free Bonus for Early Response

If you order now, we'll send you a free book, "The First Hundred Million" by E. Haldeman Julius, as long as limited supplies last. Ted Nicholas has reviewed this book. He said, "This is the very best book

(please turn to page 6)

ever written on selling. I got more tips out of it than any other marketing book I have ever read!" Ted paid $250 to get his copy of the same book from the Library of Congress! Kurt Koenig, an attendee at one of Ted's seminars heard Ted describe the book. Kurt got so excited he acquired the rights from the author's estate and arranged for a small reprint.

The author, E. Haldeman Julius, in this rare book shows you the exact advertising techniques he used to sell over 100,000,000 books. His tests reveal exactly what the public wants to buy today! This will help you structure your product offers with themes that bring in sales. This book is not available in book stores. But it is yours free if you act promptly.

Money-Back Guarantee

Review the Home Study Course for 60 days. If you are not completely satisfied for any reason, return it undamaged for a prompt and courteous refund. And keep the bonus book regardless.

Please complete the enclosed application and mail now. And thank you.

Sincerely,

B. J. Waller
President

P.S. Imagine. You get the Ted Nicholas Home Study Course on tape, MILLION DOLLAR SALES SECRETS, "*Magic Words That Bring You Riches*," plus Ted Nicholas' personal critique upon request. And all for just $477! And its guarantee for 90 days. Plus, you get a free copy of "The First Hundred Million" by E. Haldeman Julius to keep regardless.

P.P.S. Your investment may be tax deductible. Please check with your tax advisor.

© Copyright 1995 Nicholas Direct, Inc.

Nicholas Direct, Inc.
P.O. Box 877
Indian Rocks Beach, FL 33785
Telephone: (727) 596-4966

The Internet

Response on the Internet has also been very successful. We ran the same one-step ad as in space and sent the same sales letter that was sent to print ad respondents with a good conversion rate. Internet marketing will be vastly expanded as if offers more promise than any current new media.

Other marketing activities

While this chapter focuses on *paid* advertising, to generate publicity and sales on an unpaid basis, we also:

1. *Sent the book* to a list of about 400 select reviewers.

2. Sent a *news release* to print media—magazines and newspapers.

3. Sent the book to *select mail order dealers* who can produce volume sales after buying books from us on a wholesale basis.

Action to take with a new product

1. *Set a goal.* Identify exactly what you want to accomplish.

2. *Write an ad.*

3. *Create* a new product (or get the mail order rights to an existing product).

4. *Produce your advertising.*

5. *Test in print media first*—newspapers, magazines, direct mail.

6. *Create a Website* and prepare copy based on successful print tests.

7. *Possibly test T.V.*

8. *"Roll out"* based on actual results.

9. *Do no-cost PR.*

10. *Appoint dealer* to market to their audience.

11. *License* others outside the U.S.

12. *Enjoy your increased wealth*—and keep it in perspective with your health and family.

How to Prepare a Successful Mailing Kit That Transcends Language Barriers

Live samples of actual current promotions are a popular feature in this book.

Plus, based on reader comments, interest in marketing internationally is dramatically increasing.

I have some good news! This chapter will be helpful to you on both counts.

If you do it right, a successful offer in the U.S. will work as well or better in other countries. Especially in Europe and Asia. The same emotional appeals work throughout the world. And always will. Why? People everywhere have exactly the same fears and wants.

Unless you speak other languages fluently, once you prepare the copy all you need is a good translation.

Recently I prepared a mailing kit for a German client. Since it may not be mailed in the U.S. and other countries, I thought I'd take you behind the scenes. I will share the entire strategy and marketing plan.

Whether or not you intend to market in any country other than where you are based, you will be exposed to a lot of elements which can help your marketing endeavors. As you'll soon see, the mailing includes examples of several little-known techniques.

Tip: It can't be repeated often enough. The sequence in which you prepare the elements of a successful mailing is very important. I recommend you prepare them in this order:

(1) Outer Envelope

(2) Order Card or Free Trial Request

(3) letter

(4) brochure

(5) lift letter (if any)

(6) Any other element, such as description of bonuses

The following will reveal the best approach to the key elements of the mail kit, including the cover letter, recommendations to the client and a preliminary graphic layout sometimes called a "copywriter's rough." Following this are some insider tips.

Up to 5 FREE Gifts!

Answers to every manager's most pressing problem...

How to Reduce Personnel Costs and Still Comply With Germany's Tough New Labor Laws

... See inside for solution

Envelope A Front

Up to 5 FREE Gifts!

Answers to every manager's most pressing problem...

How to Profit From Today's Most Successful Personnel Secret... See inside for details

Envelope B Front

Up to 5 FREE Gifts!

Answers to every manager's most pressing problem...

How to <u>Recruit</u>, <u>Train</u> and <u>Retain</u> Honest, Desirable Employees

... See inside for details

Envelope C Front

Warning to Managers:

You Must Comply With Dangerous New Labor Laws While Holding Down Personnel Costs... See inside for solutions

Up to 5 FREE Gifts!

Envelope D Front

Free Report Reveals 7 Little Known Ways To Slash Personnel Costs... See inside for details

Up to 5 FREE Gifts!

Envelope E Front

"The Key to Business Success is Finding The Right Employees and Keeping Them"... See inside for details

Up to 5 FREE Gifts!

Envelope F Front

How to Prepare a Successful Mailing Kit 191

(Up to 5 FREE Gifts!)   Finding and managing employees successfully is one of the German manager's most pressing problem

FREE Gift #1   Protect yourself with large law poster, WE ARE A MODEL COMPANY. The 3 most Important laws affecting employees
FREE Gift #2   80 AIRTIGHT EMPLOYMENT CONTRACTS AND EMPLOYEE LETTER AGREEMENTS
FREE Gift #3   HOW TO INSPIRE WORKERS TO HAVE A PROFIT-MAKING, COST-CUTTING MINDSET!
FREE Gift #4   SECRETS OF RECRUITING PERSONNEL NO UNIVERSITY TEACHES
FREE Gift #5   7 BEST EXAMPLES OF DISMISSALS WHICH HOLD UP IN COURT

Envelope Back (all)

Graphic recommendations

1. *Envelope*. Size same as previously used. Paper color pale yellow. Black ink on main headline. Money green ink on pre-headline. Back: Money green ink headline on flap. Black ink on rest. Initially test at least three envelope versions, with strongest being A, C, and F.

2. *Free Trial Request*. Certificate-looking border. Pale green, rich-looking paper. Similar to a bank check. Black ink. This is the most important element.

3. *Brochure*. Paper: semi-gloss. Folded as previously. In full color. Headlines: largest ones *black ink*. Smaller headlines *red* and green ink. No color screens behind copy. Screening, if used, only surrounding copy. Liberal use of bright yellow in boxes. Photographs of customers and/or editors in color, smiling, eye contact with reader. No facial hair. Business attire. Size similar to that used previously.

4. *Letter*. White paper, yellow highlights as indicated. Black ink body copy, reflex blue ink signature and margin notes, with margin notes in same handwriting as signature. Logo small at end of letter. Courier typeface. Make sure black ink coverage is good. "Up to 5 free gifts" on page one should be or resemble a label.

Free Trial Request

To the personal attention of Dr. Manfred Jahrmarkt

Yes! I want to solve my personnel questions faster as well as comply with new German Labor Law. Please send me on approval for 6 weeks the 2017 page basic reference work, THE NEW HUMAN RESOURCE REFERENCE WORK FROM A TO Z. I will receive it at DM 39.80 (20% off the regular rate of DM 49.80), and the updates and supplements (80 pages each approximately 12 times a year) at 46.2 pfennigs per page. This agreement can be canceled at any time—no time limits to meet at the end of a subscription year. My two valuable gifts, the exclusive law poster "WE ARE A MODEL COMPANY" and the floppy disk, "80 AIR-TIGHT EMPLOYMENT CONTRACTS AND EMPLOYEE LETTER AGREEMENTS," are mine to keep, no matter what I decide after the free trial.

Iron-Clad Guarantee

I expressly guarantee here in black and white that requesting THE NEW HUMAN RESOURCE REFERENCE WORK FROM A TO Z involves absolutely no risk to you. You will receive the 2017 page basic reference work and then have 6 weeks time to browse through it at your leisure. If you are not completely satisfied, all you do is return it at the expense of the publishing house (Verlag Praktisches Wissen GmbH, Industriestraße 27, 77615 Offenburg) any time within these 6 guaranteed free trial weeks. Timely shipment (postmark) is sufficient to fulfill the time limit.

(signature)
Dr. Manfred Jahrmarkt
Publisher

☐ I have responded within 21 days. Please send me the following additional early bird gifts, absolutely FREE:

FREE Special Report: HOW TO INSPIRE WORKERS TO HAVE A PROFIT-MAKING, COST-CUTTING MINDSET!

FREE Special Report: SECRETS OF RECRUITING PERSONNEL NO UNIVERSITY TEACHES

FREE Special Report: 7 BEST EXAMPLES OF DISMISSALS WHICH HOLD UP IN COURT

These gifts, valued at DM 210, are FREE and are mine to keep regardless of what I decide after the free trial of the basic work.

X_____
Signature

```
Name
Address Label
```

Fax or mail this Free Trial Request to:
Verlag Praktisches Wissen GmbH, Industriestraße 27
Postfach 2505, 77615 Offenburg
Telefax: 07 81/5 98 25

Now You Can Reduce Personnel Costs And Still Comply With Germany's Tough New Labor Laws

Up to 5 FREE Gifts

Dear Friend,

One of every employer's most pressing problems is managing employees successfully.

You actually have a <u>dual problem</u> which must be solved.

First, you must <u>control</u> and often <u>reduce</u> personnel <u>costs</u>.

Second, you must avoid running into trouble with tough new labor laws. Why?

<u>A simple mistake can end up costing you a fortune</u>. Lawyers, settlement costs and fines can devastate any company.

In addition, good help is getting harder to find and retain than ever before. In the past, with plentiful candidates and lower salaries, you could get away with the old fashioned approach used by employers: "Hire fast and fire slow."

But with skyrocketing costs and burdensome regulations, it is no longer prudent to hire anyone too fast.

And when you have to get rid of an employee performing poorly, you must follow the correct procedures to avoid trouble.

Today's most successful employee policy used by smart managers is this:

This works best!

"Hire slow and fire fast"

Now, much <u>more attention</u> must be given to <u>choosing</u> the <u>right person for</u> the job. Then you must train and motivate employees so they stay with you on your team. Otherwise, they will quit.

And if the person isn't performing up to expectations, you must let them go. As fast as possible. Actually, if things aren't working out, this is also the most humane policy for the employee. He or she can quickly seek an opportunity better suited for them elsewhere. And, as you know, the longer an employee is on board, the more agonizing it is to fire them.

Answers to virtually every personnel problem you face are now yours. A completely new publication is the solution you need. It's called THE NEW HUMAN RESOURCE REFERENCE WORK FROM A TO Z. A quick reference guide, it's designed to be easy to use. It's prepared especially for the human resource manager with little time to spend on the myriad of personnel matters which come up daily.

With you permission, I'll send it to you for a <u>6-week free trial</u>. You may examine it in <u>your office and actually begin</u> applying it to your personnel matters. <u>Without risking a single pfennig</u>.

<u>Plus, you may have up to 5 free gifts valued at 210 DM</u> which are yours, regardless, just for taking a look at the 2017 page NEW HUMAN

(over)

Letter—Page 1

RESOURCE REFERENCE WORK FROM A TO Z.

Here is a brief glimpse into what you will discover:

- How to find the best applicant for the open position
- The 17 best solutions for lowering personnel costs
- Fast and sure solutions to difficult personnel questions
- Sound decision aids based on the latest decisions and laws
- When you should issue a reprimand and for what reasons—sample reprimands which will stand up in court from the use of alcohol to tardiness
- How much of your valuable time you should spend before you get rid of an employee
- Proven, legally sound sample letters and forms (even for difficult cases)
- The ideal length you should put a new employee on a probationary trial period
- How to extend the employee trial period
- How to handle an employee who abuses the privilege of calling in sick
- How to reduce supposed sick time—a checklist from actual practice tells you how
- How to fire an employee in a legal manner on the spot
- 23 legally sound methods from reprimanding to firing an employee
-  German personnel regulations organized by actual cases—immediate decision aids for daily personnel work based on the latest legal decisions and laws
- How to slash high incidental wage costs
- How you as an employer can improve your negotiating position before German labor courts, with 183 examples of which dismissals held up and which did not
- How to reliably avoid typical mistakes and pitfalls when employing social insurance-exempt help
- How to preserve your rights when dealing with

  [] health insurance companies

  [] tax authorities

  [] employees

  ...with 97 legally sound sample letters
- The 15 most efficient strategies to head off requests for raises, without hurting and demotivating your employees or even forcing them to resign

(go to page 3)

Letter—Page 2

- How to confidently handle conversations concerning criticism, with sample cases and conversation guidelines for 12 unpleasant situations
- What methods to use which reduce the number of hires which flop
- How to see through and protect yourself against the 23 tricks used by dishonest job applicants
- How to determine whether overtime or temporary help is better for the company
- How to prepare letters of reference so they cannot be contested
- How to deal with employees who are troublemakers, intriguers and gripers
- What you absolutely must include in a reprimand in case a dismissal is later necessary
- How to determine when a claim for old vacation days from the previous year is valid with airtight sample letters for each situation
- How to solve the problem of employees who are chronically latecomers, with numerous legal and psychological aids
- What obligations you have to collect taxes from employees as required by law
- How to work with freelance workers who are not employees
- → How to award workers with tax free compensation—e.g. travel, meals, free room, free board, automobiles, employee discounts, etc.
- How to decide how much vacation to give, the minimum you must provide, and how long the employee must wait
- How to prepare vacation request and approval documents that are easy to administer
- How to calculate remuneration applicable to social insurance coverage which is not covered
- → How to formulate temporary workers contracts — Caution: without the basic work, this is not easy and leads to repeated questions
- How to prepare an employment contract for spouses, frequently employed by small and medium sized companies
- How to structure an employment agreement for someone to take care of private household chores
- During a job interview, which questions get you the answers you need and which questions are not permitted
- How to prepare a help wanted ad that helps attract exactly the employee you are looking for
- How to recognize irregularities in job descriptions

(over)

Letter—Page 3

- How to garner and <u>analyze the information</u> you really need from any letter of reference
- <u>168 proven and tested sample help wanted ads</u> that help attract new employees ←7
- <u>28</u> best <u>cost-saving methods</u> of <u>settling</u> dismissal protection lawsuits out of court
- On <u>severance pay</u>, which labor courts approve <u>half a month's</u> pay per year of company employment and which demand a <u>full month</u>
- **Note** How to prepare a <u>non-binding job description</u> without going to a lot of trouble and, more important, <u>how to update</u> them without using extra employees
- How to <u>protect yourself</u> from <u>damage claims</u> from employees
- How to devise <u>profit-sharing incentives</u> for employees
- How to install a <u>business travel policy</u> which reimburses employees and which you as an employer can <u>tax deduct</u>
- How to <u>stay abreast</u> of rapidly changing <u>labor laws</u>
- When to use the "<u>general</u>" <u>income tax table</u> and when to use the "special" income tax table
- How to create a <u>private pension plan</u> that motivates and rewards loyal employees
- How to determine <u>maternity payments</u> and who pays them
- What work a <u>pregnant employee</u> must not be permitted to perform
- How to handle <u>employees from new states</u>, including registration procedures, contributions, additional earnings, pension and proofs
- How to determine <u>when retirement insurance is compulsory</u> and for whom it is <u>voluntary</u>—when a premature old-age pension is possible
- When you can dock vacation time or count the time as <u>sick days</u>
- When and how to handle the issue of a <u>Christmas bonus</u>, or decide to have one at all

Here is what readers say:

"Clear headers are particularly important so that you immediately know what the topic is about."
—(full name of person being quoted and city of residence)

"The language is very easy to understand."
—(full name of person being quoted and city of residence)

"Your services are great. I use them regularly."
—(full name of person being quoted and city of residence)

"I particularly liked the extra floppy disk with the contracts and forms."
—(full name of person being quoted and city of residence)

(go to page 5)

Letter—Page 4

"I am very satisfied with the reference work and use it often. Even my tax consultant doesn't have a better source of information."
—(full name of person being quoted and city of residence)

"We are enthusiastic. Offer this reference work to tax consultants."
—(full name of person being quoted and city of residence)

"Thank you very much for the prompt assistance during the editor's office hour. I will certainly recommend you to other people."
—(full name of person being quoted and city of residence)

"Without exception your documents are excellent. They have already been a great help to me."
—(full name of person being quoted and city of residence)

"A small reliable helper for daily use. I am very satisfied with the services of your publishing house."
—(full name of person being quoted and city of residence)

"We subscribe to your 'New Human Resource Reference from A to Z' and are also very satisfied with the content and presentation."
—(full name of person being quoted and city of residence)

"The problems which are discussed are current and presented clearly. They are a great help for these types of questions."
—(full name of person being quoted and city of residence)

"I can confirm that I easily find brief and to-the-point answers to my questions."
—(full name of person being quoted and city of residence)

Two FREE Gifts for you

Just for examining THE NEW HUMAN RESOURCE REFERENCE WORK FROM A TO Z we will send you two gifts absolutely free.

FREE Bonus Gift #1: Large law poster entitled WE ARE A MODEL COMPANY. Protect yourself. A must for every office. You can post the three most important laws covering employees in your place of business, and thus enhance relations with workers, your most important asset. Fits on all doors. Normally 10 DM, it's yours FREE.

Very useful!

FREE Bonus Gift #2: Floppy disk. 80 AIRTIGHT EMPLOYMENT CONTRACTS AND EMPLOYEE LETTER AGREEMENTS. The most used documents, agreements and contracts covering every aspect which needs to be

included in your written understandings. Press a button on your computer screen and out comes the document you need. Normally 50 DM, it's yours Free.

3 FREE Extra Bonus Gifts for "Early Birds"

If you respond now, within 21 days, as long as limited supplies last you will receive three extra bonus gifts, absolutely FREE.

Free Extra Bonus Gift #3: Special report. HOW TO INSPIRE WORKERS TO HAVE A PROFIT MAKING, COST CUTTING MINDSET! When your employees get better about being able to "think cost savings and profit," you will look great and your company will prosper as never before! Normally 50 DM, it's yours FREE.

(over)

FREE Extra Bonus Gift #4: Special report. SECRETS OF RECRUITING PERSONNEL NO UNIVERSITY TEACHES. The key to business success is finding the right employees and keeping them. Discover how and why recruiting personnel is not an administrative function. Should you recruit through employment agencies, classified ads, direct mail, referrals? Which is best for you? Get the answers. Normally 50 DM, it's yours FREE.

FREE Extra Bonus Gift #5: Special report. 7 BEST EXAMPLES OF DISMISSALS WHICH HOLD UP IN COURT. These dismissals have held up in German labor courts. Use these procedures as a guideline when you need to terminate a worker. You must do it right, as a single mistake can cost your company a fortune. Normally 50 DM, this report is yours FREE.

Mail your FREE Trial Certificate at once. Even if you don't continue the reference work, you get to keep 5 Free gifts, normally sold for 210 DM, regardless.

Guarantee—Try it for 6 weeks on approval

This I hereby guarantee in writing. You will receive THE NEW HUMAN RESOURCE REFERENCE WORK FROM A TO Z on approval. You may examine and apply any of the techniques you choose. For 6 weeks free of charge and without any risk whatsoever. If you decide to keep the reference work, you will get a 20% discount off the normal price. After the 6-week free trial, if you are not delighted, you may return the reference work and the matter will be ended. You'll have no further obligation.

In such a case (and one which I can hardly imagine), you may keep up to 5 free gifts regardless.

Don't hesitate. You have everything to gain and nothing to lose. You don't risk any money. Act now. Mail or fax your Free Trial Request today. Fax number is 078/59825. We'll rush you the complete reference work along with the free gifts within 48 hours.

Sincerely,

Bold signature

Dr. Manfred Jahrmarkt

P.S. Send your Free Trial Request today. You will receive up to 5 FREE gifts with a value of 210 DM just to preview the easy-to-use reference, THE NEW HUMAN RESOURCE REFERENCE WORK FROM A TO Z.

P.P.S. This is a time limited offer. I can only guarantee this offer for a period of 60 days. To avoid disappointment, act now.

Verlag Praktisches Wissen GmbH
Industriestraße 27
Postfach 2505
77615 Offenburg
Telefon: 07 81/5 50 50
Telefax: 07 81/5 98 25

Finally, answers to every manager's most pressing problem...

How to Reduce Personnel Costs
And Still Comply With Germany's Tough New Labor Laws

Here is your solution!

Large DIN A4 format (with 121 original-size forms, ready to be duplicated)

336 tips and examples from actual practice

105 checklists

Formulation aids for letters to employees, government agencies and courts

THE NEW HUMAN RESOURCE REFERENCE WORK FROM A TO Z

Building block system for letters of reference (for correct, legally sound letters of reference)

Practical commentary on current decisions

18 lawyers, tax consultants, personnel department heads, personnel advisors and court justices are working together for you!

6 ways you benefit:
1. Alphabetical access: Fast – reliable – even for laypersons
2. Large format (i.e., clearly organized presentation)
3. Generously spaced text presentation to break up the page (i.e., for fast comprehension)
4. Lots of subtitles (i.e., that also simplifies text comprehension and helps to maintain the train of thought)
5. Practical aids (e.g., sample texts, sample contracts, checklists and overviews) included in the text make it easier to spot important information immediately
6. The primary information is summarized again in a nutshell to permit the user to remember the conclusions correctly

Discover the strategies used by Germany's most wily lawyers.
2017 pages jam packed with valuable answers.
Carefully indexed and easy to reference and use.
Try it free for 6 weeks without risk. Receive up to 5 FREE gifts
just for testing it on a free preview basis.

(over please)

Brochure—Page 1

Find the answers you need easily with the new Findex System

The basic reference work, THE NEW HUMAN RESOURCE REFERENCE WORK FROM A TO Z, is designed for easy access with a new copyrighted method called Findex. Here is a partial glimpse at what the work contains.

- Hiring interviews
- Trial period
- Letter of reference
- Employment agreements
- Company expenses
- Business trips
- Income tax
- Maternity protection
- Social insurance
- Dismissal
- Temporary Help

- Part-timers
- Competition ban
- Wage accounting
- Vacation requests
- Unemployment payments
- Severance pay
- Retirement insurance
- Job announcements
- Sickness
- Reprimand
- Regrouping

Here are just a few difficult and common personnel questions to which you'll have an immediate solution at your fingertips:

- Do you know the 23 legally sound methods for reprimanding or firing an employee? Detailed checklist from use of alcohol to tardiness.
- How can you reduce high incidental wage costs significantly?
- How can you as an employer improve your negotiating position before German labor courts? With 183 examples of which dismissals held up and which did not.
- How do you reliably avoid typical mistakes and pitfalls when employing social insurance-exempt help?
- How do you preserve your rights when dealing with health insurance companies, tax authorities and employees? With 97 legally sound sample letters.
- What do you do when your employee claims he/she still has 3 more vacation days?
- Do you know the 15 most efficient strategies to head off requests for raises without hurting and demotivating your employees or even forcing them to turn in a resignation?
- How can you utilize personnel more effectively to do the jobs for which you pay them?
- What do you do when your employee, Peter H., calls in sick twice in one month?
- How much of your valuable time should you as the boss spend before you finally manage to get rid of an employee like Peter H.?
- Do you know how to confidently handle conversations concerning criticism? (With sample cases and conversation guidelines for 12 unpleasant situations.)
- Which methods of selection have been proven to reduce the hiring flop rate? Which methods are not worth their salt?
- How can you see through and protect yourself against the 23 tricks most frequently used by dishonest job applicants?
- What is better for the company? Have regular employees do overtime or hire temporary help?
- Why you should treat the statement "He behaved in an exemplary manner toward colleagues, superiors and subordinates" in letters of reference with extreme caution.

(go to page 3)

- How do you put troublemakers, intriguers and gripers on the shelf gracefully?
- What must absolutely be included in a reprimand so that the measure will take effect in case of dismissal?
- When does your employee have a claim to old vacation days from the previous year and when not? With airtight sample letters for every situation.
- What means do you have of bringing pressure to bear on continual latecomers? With all legal and psychological aids.
- Do you know how to formulate letters of reference effectively so that they cannot be contested? (Building block system for letters of reference shows you how with 33 sample texts.)
- What are the important differences between state and private health insurance? Practical decision aids with sample calculations.
- Exactly what obligations are you under to collect taxes from employees as required by law?
- Tax authorities want to know what non-monetary compensation your employees receive? E.g. automobiles, free room or board, even employee discounts.
- When may employees go on vacation? When are you as the responsible party permitted to forbid vacations without qualms or labor law problems?
- How much vacation time must you give employees? How long must a new employee wait?
- When does a job applicant have the right to lie?
- How can you garner the necessary information you need from letters of reference?
- How open and honest do you have to be when you fire employees?
- How do you attract capable new employees? Are you familiar with the 168 best sample help wanted ads?
- How legally binding are job descriptions? How can you easily change them without a problem or trouble?
- How do you handle tax and legal matters for freelance people who are not employees?
- Are you familiar with the 28 best cost-saving methods of settling dismissal protection lawsuits out of court?
- When are you permitted to fire someone who is sick? You'd be surprised.
- What are the 16 exceptions for which overtime on Sundays and holidays is permitted?

With THE NEW HUMAN RESOURCE REFERENCE WORK FROM A TO Z, you'll have all the answers to these questions. Plus, you'll be more relaxed and even sleep better at night!

(Include panel with 4 to 6 smiling subscriber photos making reader eye contact and name testimonials. If unavailable, use 4 to 6 photos of smiling people from editorial staff along with name and professional credentials.)

Here is How to Get a 6 Week Free Trial Without Risk And Up to 5 Valuable Free Gifts!

Just for examining THE NEW HUMAN RESOURCE REFERENCE WORK FROM A TO Z we will send you these gifts absolutely FREE.

FREE Bonus Gift #1: Large law poster entitled WE ARE A MODEL COMPANY. Protect yourself. A must for every office. You can post the three most important laws covering employees in your place of business, and thus enhance relations with workers, your most important asset. Fits on all doors. Normally 10 DM, it's yours FREE.

FREE Bonus Gift #2: Floppy disk. 80 AIR-TIGHT EMPLOYMENT CONTRACTS AND EMPLOYEE LETTER AGREEMENTS. The most used documents, agreements and contracts covering every aspect which needs to be included in your written understandings. Press a button on your computer screen and out comes the document you need. Normally 50 DM, it's yours FREE.

Iron-Clad Guarantee

I expressly guarantee here in black and white that requesting THE NEW HUMAN RESOURCE REFERENCE WORK FROM A TO Z involves absolutely no risk to you. You will receive the 2017 page basic reference work and then have 6 weeks time to browse through it at your leisure. If you are not completely satisfied, all you do is return it at the expense of the publishing house (Verlag Praktisches Wissen GmbH, Industriestraße 27, 77615 Offenburg) any time within these 6 guaranteed free trial weeks. And keep your bonus gifts regardless. Timely shipment (postmark) is sufficient to fulfill the time limit.

(signature)
Dr. Manfred Jahrmarkt
Publisher

3 FREE Extra Bonus Gifts for "Early Birds"

If you respond now, within 21 days, as long as limited supplies last you will receive three extra bonus gifts, absolutely FREE.

FREE Extra Bonus Gift #3: Special report. HOW TO INSPIRE WORKERS TO HAVE A PROFIT MAKING, COST CUTTING MINDSET! When your employees get better about being able to "think cost and profit," you will look great and your company will prosper as never before! Normally 50 DM, it's yours FREE.

FREE Extra Bonus Gift #4: Special report. SECRETS OF RECRUITING PERSONNEL NO UNIVERSITY TEACHES. The key to business success is finding the right employees and keeping them. Discover how and why recruiting personnel is not an administrative function. Should you recruit through employment agencies, classified ads, direct mail, referrals? Which is best for you? Get the answers. Normally 50 DM, it's yours FREE.

FREE Extra Bonus Gift #5: Special report. 7 BEST EXAMPLES OF DISMISSALS WHICH HOLD UP IN COURT. These dismissals have held up in German labor courts. Use these procedures as a guideline when you need to terminate a worker. You must do it right, as a single mistake can cost your company a fortune. Normally 50 DM, this report is yours FREE.

Free Trial Request

Yes! Please send me on approval for 6 weeks the 2017 page basic reference work, THE NEW HUMAN RESOURCE REFERENCE WORK FROM A TO Z. I will receive it at DM 39.80 (20% off the regular rate of DM 49.80), and the updates and supplements (80 pages each approximately 12 times a year) at 46.2 pfennigs per page. This agreement can be canceled at any time—no time limits to meet at the end of a subscription year. Please send me my free trial gifts as described above.

Name_____Company_____
Address_____
City_____Post Code _____

3 ways to order:
1. Call 07 81/5 50 50
2. Fax to 07 81/5 98 25
3. Or mail your order to: Verlag Praktisches Wissen GmbH
   Industriestraße 27
   Postfach 2505
   77615 Offenburg

Insider Tips

1. *Envelope*. The headline, or "teaser," copy on the envelope is a key factor. I always prepare the outer envelope first. Yes. Before the letter. See the six final headlines. These are crucially important. Clearly, unless the envelope is opened you have no chance to sell your product.

I usually write at least a couple of dozen and then choose three to six on the first test.

The envelope back is often wasted. Yet, it's the first thing a prospect sees. But most marketers leave it blank. Don't you waste this valuable space. Note the liberal use of the word FREE.

2. *Order form or Free Trial Request.* Most order forms tend to be boring. Yet, the main goal of a mailing is to induce an order. There are several reasons to always prepare the order form (free trial request) before you write the letter. For example, you don't risk running out of gas emotionally. Plus you are forced to clearly think through the offer. You can make it appealing enough that if a prospect decides to read the order form even without reading the letter, you can still get the order.

3. *Letter*. The headline on the letter is over 80% of the success of the mailing. As far as I'm concerned, it's everything. It can be the same as the envelope teaser, although usually I make it different.

Benefits in bullet format occupy most of the copy. Note use of margin notes, testimonials, yellow highlights, offer and call to action.

4. *Brochure*. Benefits as well as features are included. Order information is repeated in case it's passed along or separated from letter. See graphic recommendations for other tips.

5. *Bonuses*. I like including appealing free gifts. Exciting bonuses almost always improve response. I created three brand new ones. Notice the emphasis on eliciting prompt response and rewarding the buyer. Remember, in direct marketing, delay is death.

I'm sure you will be able to liberally use the principles from the mailing samples herewith to improve your response. Of course, since this is copyrighted material, you will need to prepare your own copy applicable to your products and services.

How to Profit from Public Speaking

Public speaking can be employed in a unique way—as an effective marketing tool.

It doesn't matter whether you speak occasionally or frequently.

You can profit from public speaking in many ways with the right approach.

However, in my experience, most people get nowhere near the advantages from public speaking that are possible.

This month I will discuss several keys to maximizing profits from public speaking.

Regardless of your career or business, as you grow, you'll find there are increased occasions to make presentations.

Fear of public speaking can limit growth

The number one phobia is public speaking. Indeed, one study shows 54% of Americans would rather face death than speak publicly! Think of it. The majority of people at a funeral would rather be in the casket than delivering the eulogy!

It's undoubtedly the dread of public speaking which keeps many people from developing their latent skills.

Instead, enormous human energy is spent avoiding getting up on a platform and making a presentation.

Yet, many people—millions—recognize the importance of being a good presenter.

Now, I'm not advocating everyone should aspire to be a paid public speaker. However, not being a good presenter can often stymie an otherwise promising business career.

It's often desirable, or necessary, in business to make presentations to employers, bankers and shareholders, among others.

Overcoming public speaking jitters

I used to spend sleepless nights worrying about even a short presentation before anybody.

On occasions where I was asked to speak before a business group or civic club, such as Rotary, I really panicked.

Typically this is what it was like. My heart pounded during the introduction. When I rose to speak, perspiration just poured off me, even in the dead of winter.

I had difficulty making eye contact with members of the audience. When I began to speak my voice quivered. Soon I lost my place. My God, it was such a painful experience!

These days the speaking experience is completely different. I look forward to public speaking. I no longer have butterflies. It's a pleasure to communicate to almost any group of people. Now my speeches and seminars have become a profit center. And I'm in demand as a speaker.

New contacts, friends and new clients also result from my speaking engagements.

Step-by-step guide to success as a public speaker

Here is the process which helped me develop speaking skills and which I recommend to you.

1. *Join Toastmasters*. The tips and actual speaking practice you get from Toastmasters is invaluable. Numerous professional speakers with whom I've spoken credit the development of their skills to this organization. Nothing can replace doing short impromptu presentations before a small audience of supportive fellow members.

2. *Join National Speakers Association*. NSA is the largest speakers organization in the U.S. There are about 4,500 members, most of whom are professional speakers.

At NSA workshops given by top experts in their field you'll discover how to raise the level of your skills.

You'll also benefit from seeing the top speakers in the nation in action. I've gotten so much out of NSA, I give back to this organization at every opportunity.

3. *Speak Free!* Practice makes anyone a better speaker.

At first, as an inexperienced speaker, it is highly unlikely anyone will offer to pay you. You must raise the level of your skills first.

However, the best form of practice is to speak publicly. Civic and business clubs and organizations are often seeking speakers for their local luncheons and meetings. Most have no budget to pay speakers.

Offer to speak to these groups free. Contact Rotary, Kiwanis, Lions Club, American Legion, Chamber of Commerce, etc.

You'll begin getting speaking experience. You will hone your skills. Plus, you have the chance to gain new clients. And future speaking engagements. When you become good enough, you'll also start to receive offers to be paid if that is of interest.

4. *Continually be a student of communication.* Read books and listen to tapes on the art of public speaking and you will constantly learn and grow. Good speakers are made and not born.

The best public speakers in history in nearly every instance overcame great difficulties before they mastered their craft. For example:

Winston Churchill—One of my favorites, he had a serious stuttering problem, which he overcame after struggling with it for years. Nothing came to him naturally. All his best known speeches were not spontaneous. They were the result of hours of practice.

Demosthenes—The famed Greek philosopher and orator conquered a severe stutter in an unusual way. He practiced speeches by the sea with his mouth full of pebbles.

Abraham Lincoln—The former President was extremely shy in his youth. He became a powerful public speaker by developing his skills as a debater.

Zig Ziglar. This great storyteller honed his communicating skills by first becoming a very successful door-to-door cookware salesman. Later, he started doing short presentations for other salespeople.

Every good speaker with whom I've ever been on the platform is continuously working on refining their skills. Of course, this includes me. When I listen to my tapes I see much room for improvement. But that's also one of the great challenges of public speaking. You can always be better.

5. *Continue to develop your expertise* When you become an acknowledged expert in any field and your topic is of interest to others, speaking invitations will increase.

Remember a proverb recommended "Read just one hour a day on any subject. You will become proficient on that topic in three years. Within five years you can become a world class expert".

6. *Give more content to audience than is expected.* People are hungry for a lot more useful content than many speakers provide. The old style motivational speech is probably on its way out.

Tip: *Provide valuable written information and* give it away free. *This underused strategy greatly multiplies the impact and remembrance value of your presentation.*

Your booklet or special report should contain information of immediate value to your audience.

Your written material should contain your name, address, telephone, fax and email numbers. If you do a good job on the presentation, prospective clients will contact you afterwards. Sometimes years later.

Enhanced presentation skills help any leader

Whether you head up a civic club on a volunteer basis, are a sales person, professional, executive, or run a business, the better you communicate, the more effective you'll be.

Numerous situations arise daily which are enhanced by a higher level of presentation skills. Effectively presenting ideas to your bank, colleagues, employees, club members, government agencies such as the IRS, even your family, can be very important to your career and life.

Using seminars to enhance your business

Conducting *free seminars* which lead to paid ones is a proven technique.

You can give an evening, half-day program on a subject upon which you are qualified.

Some examples of topics being presented are:

- Retirement planning
- Painless dentistry
- Hair transplantation
- Commodity and stock investing
- Plastic surgery
- Tax savings
- Asset protection
- Real estate investment
- Small business opportunities
- Estate planning
- Medicare and Medicaid
- Auto leasing

Tip: *Be yourself. Be honest. Be real. Speak from your heart.*

When you deliver good presentations, once attendees are comfortable with you, many benefits will accrue.

Of course, you may immediately get new business from members of your audience.

Or, you will find members of your audience refer their friends or customers to you.

Again, the key is to do a good job in your presentation. Strive to keep it lively and energetic. Filled with *actionable information.*

You may be satisfied simply raising your presentation skills to a new level using the tips so far. You may not be interested in cashing in by making money from speaking.

But if you would like to cash in on the opportunities, here is how to **break into big money public speaking**

Perhaps the fastest and most direct way to get into paid speaking is to follow this model.

A. Conduct a free seminar in your field. Give real value. For example, it can be an evening or half-day program.

B. At the end of the program, offer a longer follow-up seminar which is more in-depth.

In essence, here is the gist of what you might say at the end of your free program.

> "Now you've spent _____ hours with me where I've been sharing my insights on _____. I've included all the information I could pack into the limited time we've had together. I trust this information has been of value to you.
>
> "Many attendees have expressed an interest in further information.
>
> On *(date)* I'll be returning to this area and conducting a more in-depth seminar entitled *(similar subject)* . [The follow-up seminar can be from 2-4 days.]
>
> "If you'd like to attend, we have limited seating available. Here is a seminar reservation form. If you enroll today you can save $_____ off the regular seminar fee."

If your audience is pleased and has gotten a lot out of your presentation, a significant percentage (e.g., 20%) will come to your follow-up program.

To succeed as a professional speaker, don't make the classic mistake

Most professional public speakers are not rich. Even among the big names in speaking circles, less than two percent make a six figure income. As far as I know, none are millionaires from speaking alone.

Why? They position themselves as public speakers. In my view, this is a serious mistake.

To succeed in a big way as a public speaker, you must discover how to *leverage your message*.

Would you rather speak 1,000 times to an audience of 100? Or once to an audience of 100,000?

When I ask professional speakers who come to my seminars this question, they all would rather *present fewer times to more people.* Wouldn't you?

The killer for public speakers is the logistics and wear and tear of travel. Nearly everyone dreads the hassles of flying, hotels, etc.

Plus, suppose you became ill or injured and can't get to your engagements? Your income completely stops.

There is a complete different approach you can use. Position yourself as—***Speaker, Inc.!***

Think of yourself as a *communicator of messages* instead of as a professional *speaker*.

The key to big money as Speaker, Inc. is *passive income*.

You can earn money from passive sources whether or not you speak. Books, tapes, CD ROMS, royalties, newsletters, infomercials on T.V. and radio, on the Internet, or writing advertising copy?all are passive sources.

I view all the foregoing as *message delivery systems*.

What you should be doing is simply "rebroadcasting" your message over and over again. You employ all the message delivery systems you can.

The copy on the jacket of my book MAGIC WORDS THAT BRING YOU RICHES refers to me as *"the highest paid communicator per word in the world."*

Can I justify such a claim? I'll give you some facts and you decide. For the written word, I often receive $500,000 to as much as $1,000,000 and more in royalty income for writing a simple 1000 word ad. The ad takes me about a week to prepare. That's $500 to $1000 per word!

Actually, $500 per word is not my top rate. In fact, I've generated as much as $4,000,000 for a 1000 word ad. That's $4,000 per word. And I still earn passive income from ads I've written 10 and 15 years ago. Plus, of course, royalties from my 14 books.

Compare this income with that of a successful author of books, such as James Michener or Stephen King. These authors may earn a million plus on a book. But they will need to work on it for perhaps one or two years!

In leveraging my speaking appearances, here is how I do it. My typical seminar is audio and video taped. My presentation at the seminar, therefore, becomes a product. After the event, I sell the product for years. When I sell 10,000 units of a seminar on tape for about $300 using direct marketing techniques, I generate $3,000,000 in income. Are you beginning to see how I "package" my message differently than do most speakers?

Even the pros make this tragic mistake

A few years ago I spoke at a marketing seminar. There were eleven other speakers. I sold over $100,000 worth of books and tapes on the spot. (I'm not going to even count future consulting fees and joint ventures, etc., in this discussion.)

Some of the other speakers shared their sales results. From what I could see, combined they sold very few books, tapes and consulting services.

Understand, the speaking faculty was as good as it gets. Some of the biggest names in speaking were there, public speakers at the top of their profession, as they should be. However, in my opinion, they did not focus on the passive income side of communications.

What was the difference between the speakers who sold product and those who didn't?

Candidly, the reasons were in positioning and strategy.

1. Sales occur when your presentations are packed with *actionable content*. Most of the other speakers were great at motivation. But they didn't focus as much on how to actually use their content. I feel audiences today want to be motivated and entertained. But, in addition, they want the content to be immediately usable in their business and personal lives.

2. I enthusiastically presented special offers—for tapes and newsletters, etc. Indeed, I consider it an obligation to my audience to offer resources for anyone who wants to get deeper into my work. Direct marketing is a broad topic. Of course, I could only touch on the possibilities during the presentation. Therefore, if one wants to engage in further study, more resources become almost a necessity.

Success with products begins with how you think about them. Your attitude comes across to your audience.

Most of the legendary speakers who had a product to offer, to my surprise, didn't even describe it enthusiastically. In fact a couple of them seemed to *apologize for having a product available!*

Of course, the audience quickly picked up on this attitude.

Even more surprising is that some speakers didn't even have a product to offer at all.

A few advanced speaking tips I learned from the late Bill Gove

The *number one error* speakers make is *speaking too fast*. So, to immediately improve your speaking technique:

1. *Slow down.* More of your message will be heard, understood, and remembered.

2. *Modulate your voice.* Do not use the same voice level. Vary from soft, even a whisper, to a medium, then to stronger voice level.

3. *Pause.* Most speakers are scared to death of any pause or silence. So they talk fast, filling all silent space. However, a well-timed pause can be extremely effective, especially to help highlight a major point. So use the pause frequently.

4. *Tell stories.* Illustrate your major points with short interesting stories. People love hearing things in stories to which they can relate.

More tips on conducting seminars

Here is some of what I've learned about doing successful seminars:

- Run seminars during *weekdays* for *corporate employees*, when the company is paying.

- Run *seminars* on *nights and weekends for entrepreneurs*, when they are paying.

- *Direct mail* is usually the best medium for attracting attendees to a seminar on a specialized topic.

- Radio, TV and newspapers can be effective if you offer a general topic.

- The *longer the duration* of your program, the *longer the lead time needed*. Of course, participants need to plan their schedule to attend. For example, if you offer a five-day program, your invitations should be in the hands of your prospects at least 9 months, and up to a year, in advance.

    A one-day program works well 8-12 weeks in advance. However, they can work with just a week's notice, especially if they are invited and excited during a free "preview."

- Your *letter* of invitation is the most important piece of sales literature. Letters pull more than brochures, although you can use both. You must *stress the benefits* attendees will derive.

- *Cancellation policy*. Should anyone signed up need to cancel for any reason, the policy which works best is a credit toward a future seminar. Of course, this must be stated in your reservation form.

- *Additional speakers* who are well-known experts on aspects of the main topic presented can help attract participants.

It's better to engage a great speaker who has good information than a poor speaker with great information. If a speaker bores your audience, no matter how good the content, attendees will not be pleased.

Early on I had some embarrassing moments. I invited speakers to my seminars who were recommended but who I hadn't heard speak myself. And they bombed.

Tip: *Never invite a speaker on anyone's recommendation. You personally should have heard them speak, and liked their style and content.*

- Put the *best speakers* on the agenda *first and last*. People long remember those they hear first. And also the speaker heard last. The last speaker should be the best of all presenters.

- *Choose "low-maintenance" speakers*. Do not invite "prima donna" types who want constant attention, and are always complaining. It's just not worth the hassle.

  As with all of life, choose people you can trust and who keep their word. Plus, the best speakers to work with are also the most giving to their audience. The rare, though ideal, is a speaker who does everything possible to make your seminar a success.

- *Choose good hotels* that have their act together. Your program will go so much better if the hotel has the reputation of being on the ball with regard to all the important details. These include lighting, sound system, seating, heat/air conditioning, food and beverage service, etc. Your events can be a pleasure, or a nightmare, depending on service.

- *Register* your *attendees one hour in advance* of the seminar. You need a competent and businesslike staff of 1-3 or more people. Of course, this depends on size of the event. Issue name tags to all attendees.

- *Check out your meeting room* at least one hour before the event. The day before is better should you need to make major adjustments.

- *Review details*. lighting, sound, seating, temperature (too cool is better than too hot!), podium, tables, easels, overhead projector, blackboard—everything needed to make the event go as smoothly as possible. As has been said, the genius is in the details.

- Be sure to have all attendees, including speakers, *sign a release* if you are taping the event and plan to sell video and/or audio recordings of the seminar later.

Quick summary

1. Working on your skills and you will become a better speaker.
2. Join Toastmasters, NSA, do free speeches. Do free speeches. Read. Listen to tapes. Attend seminars. Study communications. Write a book.
3. Give more. Deliver more actionable content than expected.
4. You can leverage your message by operating as Speaker Inc. Use all the message delivery systems available to you.
5. You can build large passive income. Create products such as books, video and audio tapes, royalties, T.V. and radio infomercials, sell on the Internet.
6. Be yourself. Reveal yourself. Speak to, not at, the audience from your heart.
7. Seminars can become a big money maker for you.

Benefits of being a better presenter

By improving your public speaking skills, you will gain many benefits. You will increase self-confidence and build self-esteem. Your career in any field will be enhanced.

Interested in big profits from public speaking? If you get into conducting seminars and do it right, you can make big money. The seminar business is not easy. But the opportunities for those who do it right are huge.

And, it's not crowded at the top. Only a handful of people in the U.S. and other countries in which I do seminars do an outstanding job. Plus, you'd be surprised. Few presenters actually "walk the talk."

The market is always hungry for more good presenters who really speak honestly from their heart.

I look forward to hearing about your well-received speeches and seminars.

Secrets of Writing a Book That Sells

Ever thought about writing a book? If so, you are not alone. Nearly everyone I know has considered the possibility at one time or another.

The good news is, I believe everyone has at least one good book inside them. You don't have to be a great writer, or even a good one, either. The reality—if you can speak, you can write a book!

I'm going to give you some tips about writing a book and suggestions that increase the chances it will sell and that you will make money from it. For the discussion, I'll focus on non-fiction.

What happens with most books

First, let's take a look at the process of how most books are written. The author decides to write a book on a particular topic. It's usually a subject the writer knows a lot about.

A long effort involving months, or even years, is spent laboring over the manuscript. The chapters are written sequentially.

Finally, the book is completed.

A clever title is chosen that is meaningful only to the author. Little thought or attention is given to the book title.

Then the author has to make some decisions.

Who is going to publish the book? How will the book be distributed and sold?

Writers tend to submit unpublished books directly to "trade" publishers within the New York publishing establishment.

What happens at a typical publishing company?

The manuscript will probably not be read. The usual policy is to reject *all* incoming unsolicited manuscripts, especially from first-time authors.

The odds are, the book never gets published. Out of approximately 750,000 manuscripts submitted to U.S. publishers, only 90,000 are published, about 1 in 8.

As to a six or seven figure advance payment that you read about occasionally, what really happens in most cases? The typical advance for an unpublished author is modest, usually $1,000 to $5,000, with rare exceptions.

Contrary to popular belief, out of those published, only 5%, or about 3,500 books in all of the U.S., sell out of their first printing. The rest, 95%, are on the shelves, making little or no significant money for the author or publisher.

I don't recommend the foregoing procedure. There are other choices in publishing a book. These include:

1. *Self-publishing*. This is where the author publishes the book.
2. *Combined publishing*. This can often be the best solution. A conventional publisher handles distribution in bookstores, libraries and schools. The author handles direct marketing via print ads, direct mail, card decks, radio, TV and the Internet.

Common myths about book publishing

To achieve success, you need to forget practically everything conventional wisdom has taught you about book publishing!

Let's look at several common publishing myths.

Myth	Reality
1. Bookstores are the only source of volume book sales.	About 50%, roughly half, of all books sold in the U.S. are direct marketed via print ads or by mail.
2. A bookstore is the best place to sell books.	Bookstores are one of the worst places to sell books. You are competing for shelf space with over 70,000 other titles, so it's tough to get attention. Successful independent publishers tolerate bookstores, but do not depend on them.
3. Writing a book is the primary task, after which you can sit back and watch the receipts roll in.	At most, preparing the book is 10% of the task of a successful publishing endeavor. The other 90% of the focus must be on *marketing*.
4. It's tough to get on TV radio to promote a book.	With a well-written book, a good and title, and a subject of interest to a large segment of the population, TV and radio bookings are surprisingly easy.
5. It costs a fortune to publish a book.	You can publish 5,000 copies of a typical book as well as test ads and mail for less than $15,000. If you sell them all at $20, you can gross $100,000.

Secrets of Writing a Book that Sells 223

6. A good book will sell itself once published and out in print.	Rarely does any book achieve volume sales without continued marketing efforts on the part of the author.
7. Consumers buy books based on publisher's reputation.	Consumers don't care who the publisher is. Books are bought based on interest in the subject matter.
8. People don't judge a book by its cover.	People *do* judge a book by its cover. It's a most important marketing tool.
9. To be a successful author, you must write the book.	Not true. Many popular and successful books are ghostwritten collaborations.
10. Self-published books never become best sellers.	Numerous best sellers have been self-published. A few examples include:

- *Celestine Prophecy* (#1 NY Times Best Seller) by James Redfield
- *Erroneous Zones* (#1 NY Times Best Seller) by Dr. Wayne Dyer
- HOW TO FORM YOUR OWN CORPORATION WITHOUT A LAWYER FOR UNDER $75 by yours truly, with over 1,000,000 copies in print (working on the second million!)

Tip: *If you enjoy verbal communication better than sitting down with a notebook or computer, you can dictate your book on tape and have it transcribed. Many find this simple technique a time saver.*

Publishing—The Ideal Business

It will probably come as no surprise to you that I favor self-publishing as the best method. Why? Partly out of necessity. Nine publishers turned down my first book!

But, there is another reason, too, that I backed into. Before I published my first book, I had started 18 companies in a variety of fields. These included candy and ice cream (retailing), cosmetics, real estate and franchising.

I've always searched for the ideal business. Perhaps no business could ever be ideal in every respect. But the one that comes closest is publishing of books, tapes, CD's and other information products.

Here are the main reasons why I believe publishing is nearest the ideal:

- Products are easy to "manufacture." You can get books, tapes, etc. produced in almost any city in America.
- There is a *high perceived* value for information. You have *substantial* markups. Profit margins can be high: from 10 to as high as 30 times cost is not uncommon. It's not the paper or the video tape people buy; it's the information.
- The trends all point to growing opportunities in the future in our "information age."
- You can live and operate from anywhere in the world. The business is completely portable, movable anywhere. This gives you an unsurpassed lifestyle.
- You have no competition. Your products are copyrighted. They are proprietary, cannot be copied and belong to you alone.
- Your market is the entire planet.
- The business is not capital intensive. You can start with as little as $600.

- Business is not dependent on age, sex or nationality.
- You can operate with few or no employees.
- You have less government regulation in publishing than probably any other business, due mostly to freedom of the press—a constitutional guarantee.
- You are doing business with intelligent, high-quality people for the most part.
- You are providing a wonderful human service by educating others and thus making the world a better place. You will be proud to be a publisher.
- And, when you sell the business, it's one of the most attractive and, therefore, very saleable businesses.

Secrets of preparing a successful book

Before you write a single word in your book, here is what I recommend you do.

Step I—Create a book *title*. The title *is extremely important!* Think of the title as a *headline for the book*. Don't try to be clever or cute. A great title can simply be the biggest benefit derived from your book from the reader's point of view. Write lots of titles. I wrote 217 before I chose HOW TO FORM YOUR OWN CORPORATION WITHOUT A LAWYER FOR UNDER $75.

Tip: Pass this test. *If the book title were used as a headline for an editorial, would it be strong enough to entice you to read the article? If not, change it immediately!*

Step II—Prepare a detailed outline for the book. Write each chapter title in the form of a headline.

Step III—Write an ad selling the book!

Writing an ad forces you to think through the book from the reader's point of view. Very few authors ever do this. That's why the majority of books are a "me" oriented ego trip and thus incredibly dull and boring for the reader.

Preparing an ad for your not-yet-written book is the most important and powerful recommendation I could ever make to any aspiring writer. For example, I wrote the ad for my latest book, MAGIC WORDS THAT BRING YOU RICHES, one year before I wrote it. When I sent the ad to my friends and they immediately wanted to buy the book, I knew I had a winner!

Besides making the finished book more "reader friendly" and thus more saleable, there are several other important advantages writing an ad provides, including:

A. A good ad is filled with benefits. As you write the book, you will be forced to include many benefits useful to the reader to make it live up to all you promise.

B. Your ad copy can become the basis for your book jacket copy.

C. Your ad copy can become the basis of pre-publication news releases and articles about the forthcoming book.

D. You can run your ad or send copies to prospects for the purpose of pre-publication sales for the book. Thus, you can generate substantial revenue even before the book is printed and the printing bill becomes due. Simply make a "pre-publication" offer.

How to choose a book topic

The best place to start looking for a good topic is to first search your life and experience. Write about what you know. The odds are good that a lot of people would like to know what you know.

Another important technique is to write about subjects of great interest to you, with the help of research. The more passionate you are about your subject, the better the book.

Once again, keep this in mind. "If you read on any topic for just one hour a day, you can become an expert in three years. In five years you can become a world expert!"

Surprisingly, most aspiring authors I meet have adopted the habits of today's video generation. They don't read enough. Instead, they spend as much as 25 1/2 hours a week in front of the TV, and read less than an hour a week, just like most of the population.

In my view, you can't be a successful writer unless you also spend the necessary time reading. Plus, reading great books is the best low-cost way to interact with many of the best minds in the world.

Ideas for good book topics can also come by doing a lot of *active listening*. You'll discover what interests people and what they gripe about. A successful book can be compared to a successful entrepreneur. Both solve human problems, the basis of business success.

How to get the book produced

Here are the key points:

1. Get a copyright

2. Get an ISBN and Library of Congress number

3. Typeset the manuscript

4. Arrange for the photography

5. Print the book

For guidance on these items and others, see my title, HOW TO PUBLISH A BOOK & SELL A MILLION COPIES. You can get a copy of the e-book by going to:

http://www.publishabookandsellamillioncopies.com

Don't let the production side of a book intimidate you. It's no problem. The simple truth is, producing the book once it's written is the easy part. Also, there are lots of people, such as book printers, all over the U.S. who are only too happy to help you just by making a few phone calls.

That's why I focus here on marketing information, which is far more valuable and the hardest to come by. It's your book marketing program, not production, that determines your level of success.

The all-important book cover or jacket

Before the book is produced, you'll need to make some decisions on size and whether it's hard or soft cover.

Generally I recommend most books be printed in *hardcover*. The perceived value is greater. For perhaps one or two dollars more in costs for hardcover versus softcover, you can charge a price of $5 to $50 more!

> ***Tip:*** *One simple method of producing a book which you can be proud of is this. Go to a bookstore and buy a book whose size, design, and paper weight appeals to you and use it as a model. Just ask your printer to give you a price quotation on producing your book in a similar style.*

Designing the book jacket

The jacket copy and design are extremely important. There are situations, such as in bookstores, where impulse sales are possibilities. Also, while less important to a mail order buyer, an exciting cover invites pass along sales, gifts, and special volume sales to book clubs, newsletter publishers, associations, cataloguers and premium users.

Elements of a good book jacket include:

1. Title
2. Powerful graphics
3. Benefits of the book used as subheads or bullets
4. Brief description of contents
5. Author information
6. Comments from experts or well-known readers

Most book titles, jackets and copy are incredibly dull and boring.

Why? They are often prepared either by the author from a "me" point of view instead of the reader's, or by an editor who doesn't have a marketing focus.

Think of a *book jacket* as *an ad for the book*, a crucially important part of the marketing program.

1. The title of a book has a large responsibility. It should draw attention, make the book stand out from all others, telegraphically communicate what it's about, and cause a browser to want to buy it.

2. The jacket graphics ideally help to:

   A. Telegraphically communicate the title. It should be large and bold enough to be easily read, even when the book is reduced in ads to the size of a postage stamp.

   B. Dramatize any photography that is used.

   C. Help make copy easy to read. Avoid sans-serif typefaces, except possibly in the title. Also avoid overusing reverse printing (black and other colors with white printing). Instead, use black and dark colors on white or light backgrounds.

Tip: *Work with a graphic designer experienced with books who can supply you examples of previous work you really like. Expect to pay somewhere in the vicinity of $1,000 to $2,000. This could be the best investment you'll ever make in your book.*

3. *Benefit of the book.* Incorporate in the form of bulleted points at least five or six benefits a reader will get from your book. These should come from the ad you've previously written.

Tip: *An effective marketing technique is to include after each bullet point a book page number, i.e. "See page 141", etc*

4. *A brief description* of the book's contents should be printed beginning on the inside front flap of your book jacket. If you've done a good job on the ad, you can use this copy as its basis.

5. *Author information.* Include a photo, background and qualifications of yourself or the author if it's someone other than you.

Tip: *Have a professional photo done in conservative business attire. Avoid casual clothes. For greater effect, always look into the camera, having the effect of eye contact with reader. A sincere smile is more effective than a serious look.*

6. *Comments from experts or well-known readers* can help. Getting "blurbs" to use as testimonials for your jacket is not usually a problem. It's often as simple as asking an expert if they'd review and comment on your manuscript. Most people tend to feel flattered and/or glad to help. Ideally, what you want to strive for is to have three or so well-known experts on the book's subject quoted on your book jacket. Of course, get permission to use the quotes.

Tip: *A simple way to get a usable quote from a busy expert is to send them one chapter on a subject of their expertise for their suggestions, as well as a quote. Offer to list them in your* *acknowledgments and to send them a gift of six copies when the book is printed. You'll often get some helpful editorial assistance plus a fan of your book, which can help sell a lot of copies!*

To illustrate how important I consider the book jacket to be, here is my current procedure. For my forthcoming books, after I write the ad and before the book is written, I have the basic jacket designed (the blurbs are not yet included). The book jacket is a powerful living tool to assist me in discussions with distributors, bookstore buyers, libraries, schools, foreign publishers, licensees, book clubs, etc.

Perhaps the most important function of a book jacket designed early for me is personal. Every time I look at it, I get excited. It helps keep me motivated to prepare a great book that lives up to that fabulous cover!

No authors of whom I'm aware use all these unconventional little known but highly effective strategies. Try them for yourself. You will be delighted with the results! I'd appreciate hearing your success story!

So You Want to do an Infomercial!

In this chapter I'll discuss what may be the most powerful as well as glamorous form of advertising—an infomercial.

Just what is an infomercial? In case you are not familiar with the term, an infomercial is industry jargon for a long form commercial.

The total length of a typical infomercial on TV, including announcements, is 30 minutes.

As you'll see, the investment involved to do an infomercial can be substantial. But if you own an infomercial that is successful, you have an asset that can earn millions in a very short time.

A brief history

Long-form TV commercials have been around for some time, approximately 30 years. You may recall seeing some of the earlier ones. They ran from approximately 5 to 20 minutes and featured slicers, appliances, utensils such as knives and various gadgets. One of the talents whose infomercials you may have seen were pioneered by Al Eikoff (actually Al Eikoff's advertising goes back to radio in 1947). Then came others, such as the real estate promoters who helped pioneer the sale of tapes and seminars.

Today the infomercial marketing business is huge. Sales this year are projected to be over 7 *billion dollars*. Many major corporations such as Volvo, Oldsmobile, Charles Schwab, New York Life, Merrill Lynch, American Express, etc., are marketing via infomercials.

Today's TV infomercials feature a variety of products and personalities. Tony Robbins, Fran Tarkenton, Victoria Jackson, Susan Powter, Kathy Smith, Kevin Trudeau, Bruce Jenner, and my old friend Joe Sugarman of BluBlocker fame, are but a few of the people who owe a big percentage of their present fame and fortune to their exposure on TV.

I did one of the first long form commercials for a book in 1984. It was 22 minutes long. And very successful. The product was my book HOW TO FORM YOUR OWN CORPORATION WITHOUT A LAWYER FOR UNDER $75. It ran mostly on what was then called the Financial News Network.

That first infomercial I did is downright primitive by today's standards. Plus, it's embarrassing every time I view it as the haircut, tie, suit and shirt are hopelessly out of style! The format is simply two people talking with each other. Just two "talking heads" as the media people like to say. Today much more visual action is the norm.

Since this early infomercial, I've consulted on infomercials for clients. Plus, I've produced three others for my own products and services. Of the last three I've done, one flopped. And one broke even. Happily I ran one for several years which was a success! Currently, we're planning to run it in the European and Asian market.

Two big obstacles

1. As with all advertising, the *biggest cost* is *waste circulation*. On television at any given time you have *large numbers* of people who will never be prospects for your product.

However, when you buy air time, of course you must pay for this waste circulation anyway. So, for starters you must have a product or service with *mass appeal*.

If your target market niche is too narrow, it's unlikely TV will work for you. You probably won't be able to afford paying for the excessive waste circulation. (There is an exception to this on TV. It's possible to do niche marketing on TV with demographics as few as 20,000 people, but it involves highly specialized "niche buying" of TV time. I know of one case where a general doctor was able to profitably advertise five days a week for a two-year period.)

With small, narrow audiences you must more closely *target* your marketing *message*. In niche markets it's more cost effective to reach the likely prospects for your product with highly targeted media such as direct mail, and card decks. Or as space ads in magazines, newspapers and trade journals.

2. The second big problem on TV is the *clicker* (remote control). The typical TV viewer has a clicker in hand or close by. If your infomercial bores the viewer or doesn't capture and hold the viewer's attention within the first few seconds, click, and your message is gone!

That's a big reason why most successful infomercials have a lot of exciting action, celebrities, interesting backgrounds, cut-aways and special effects.

What are your chances of success?

The bad news for infomercials is the success rate is very low. Just 1 in 10 make money according to industry experts. In spite of big budget programs, even by industry giants, 9 out of 10 infomercials tested are flops.

Huge "home runs," defined as those which pull $80,000,000 or more in sales, are 1 in 30. There are a few really "hot" entrepreneurs who have made a profit with 1 in 5 infomercials. Therefore, it is possible to beat the formidable odds.

What will be your investment?

Of course, there is no simple answer to the kind of investment required. It depends on the location, format of the show, use of celebrities and other talent. While in the past there have been some successful infomercials costing as little as $25,000-$35,000, I know of none today that costs less than $150,000. The lower range can be $150,000 to $350,000. The big companies are investing as much as 2-3 million dollars. The TV medium with the high risks and relatively low chance of success is obviously not for the fainthearted!

But what if you succeed?

The good news is that if your infomercial succeeds, you can earn millions on the "front end" in a very short time. If you are the on-camera personality, you will also become a famous celebrity. In addition, you will build a mailing list to whom you can offer a stream of new products. And you can rent out your list for even more profits.

Plus, you will develop a retail demand for your product. You can switch to selling through retail outlets later when your infomercial stops working. Retail sales can be from 3 to 10 times results on TV.

And there's more! You can repeat the process in country after country. Virtually every place in the world is now, or soon will be, offering opportunities to run your infomercial. If it works on TV in the U.S., there is better than a 90% chance you will succeed in foreign markets with the same program. All you usually have to do is make some changes in price and narrative content.

Plus, overseas offers can sometimes work when they do not in the U.S. Buyers tend to be less sophisticated with lower sales resistance.

Marketing goals you can achieve

Infomercials, of course, can be used to directly sell products and services on the show itself. Other possibilities which are working include:

Lead generation for follow-up by phone and mail. This can work successfully for products and services costing $300 or more, such as business opportunities.

Seminar seats—A free seminar at which paid seminars and tapes are sold is a proven format.

Retail sales—You can attract prospects to retail stores and car dealerships with a good infomercial.

Is there a formula for success?

With infomercials, as with all creative endeavors, there is more than one way to succeed. As the great saying goes—there is more than one way to get to heaven!

Perhaps the best way to help you is to share how I and some of the other successful infomercial entrepreneurs approach the matter.

Because of the cost and risk, *TV* is *not* the best medium on which to *launch* new products and services.

But a TV infomercial can be an *excellent direct marketing* medium for a *proven* product.

Therefore, if you take products and services which are direct marketed successfully in non-TV media like print or direct mail, you can often build on this success via TV. This is providing, as previously mentioned, the product has a wide enough appeal.

Your creative task on converting your success on other media is this. Take the *essence* of what is working, *especially the emotional hot buttons* you are already pushing, and transfer it to the TV screen!

What you are doing is capitalizing on that elusive factor you know already exists within your offer—**a known constant!**

Before the foregoing confuses anyone, let me clarify further.

I've found that sales appeals are transferable from one medium to another. As a marketer you know customers buy your product or service for *emotional reasons*.

When you clearly know what emotion your message is stirring a customer to *make a buying decision*, you possess a valuable *asset*. Properly managed, this asset can be *more valuable than gold*!

A case history

Here is some background to my most successful infomercial.

The forerunner to the U.S. TV show was a successful space ad I wrote that ran in the US and the UK.

The name of the product featured is the informed book, MAGIC WORDS THAT BRING YOU RICHES along with some special reports and cassettes included as free bonuses. Of course the title of an infomercial is crucially important. The successful book title is also the name of the TV show.

The entire narrative of the show was derived almost entirely from the space ad. Most important is exactly the same benefits are stressed.

Of course, on television you can markedly increase the drama of the words used when you add the power of voice inflections and video pictures and images.

The importance of testimonials

As with space advertising and direct mail, *testimonials* are extremely powerful credibility builders on TV. Perhaps even more so than other media.

There is simply nothing that can replace the actual real life stories from the minds and hearts of real human beings who are communicating their experience with your product.

What was included on my infomercial was simply the interviews of some of my long term clients who were attending a large seminar I held in Tampa last year. These fine people simply related their real life experiences with my books, tapes and other materials.

Format of the show

We decided that the most exciting way to dramatize the products offered is to feature me presenting a real seminar. (We decided against employing a Hollywood actor to be spokesperson since the products offered would be entirely my work.) There is a special quality in a live seminar that can't be matched in a studio.

Strategy of the offer

Our goal from the outset was to take the essence of what is working in print and expand the audience for my work on TV. Of course, a new mailing list would be generated.

Another part of the strategy is to open the audience for products and services offered by my company, Nicholas Direct, such as audio and video tape sets, and seminars.

The idea was to give a new market of people a "taste" of the proven principles I teach at an affordable price. As with all my products, the idea is not to sell just one time but to build an ongoing, *continuing relationship*.

Price tests

We decided to offer a package of products including an audio tape set, three video tapes and my book, MAGIC WORDS THAT BRING YOU RICHES.

The price points we chose to test were a three-payment plan of $29.95, three payments of $39.95 and three payments of $49.95. (Notice I did not use a 7 here as an ending digit as 5 works better when you say it out loud!)

$39.95 was the most profitable price.

Want to be part of the infomercial's success?

If you believe, as I do, that there is no wasted energy in the universe—what goes around comes around!—we could use your assistance. Your role: just share your success with others!

Let's assume my work has already made a measurable difference in your income and/or lifestyle. We are always on the lookout for

"It Amazed My Friend... I Said Two Simple Words. And We Were Escorted to the Finest Table in the Restaurant!"

And you'll never guess what they are! Yes, knowing the right words to say will get you everything you want in life

I'll never forget the look on her face. Pure joy!

You've surely had this experience. You make dinner reservations. You are taken to your table. Inevitably it's in a poor location. Usually by the kitchen where it's noisy. Or by the drafty front door. Oddly enough this often happens, even when the restaurant is not busy. It used to happen to me all the time. Until...

I learned the secret. Now I always get the very best table, wherever I go.

Certain Words Are Magic

One day while on vacation, it hit me like a bolt of lightning! Not only special treatment in restaurants, but all the good fortune I enjoy happens for just one reason. Because of words. Simple ones.

My name is Ted Nicholas. As a writer and speaker, I've been fascinated with words and phrases all my life. I've been refining these words for years. I've taught friends to say them. The same remarkable results happen to them.

No one is misled. Every word is truthful. Best of all, these words work for anyone.

Knowing the right words to say are responsible for my earning millions. As much as $3,500,000 in a single year. Getting 13 best-selling books published. Owning two, million dollar homes. Driving a new Mercedes convertible. And traveling throughout the world.

Think of it. I'm a college dropout. I began my career with no writing or speaking skills. No money. No contacts. No wealth, friends or relatives. No special privileges of any kind. And remarkable things have happened. All because of the power of these words.

Magic Words Will Change Your Life

I've decided to share these secrets for the very first time in my new book. I'll give you every word And to whom. In all types of situations which you face daily. You will then be in a position to enhance your life beyond what you've ever imagined. My book is called MAGIC WORDS THAT BRING YOU RICHES.

I know the book title sounds almost too good to be true. A little skeptical? I would be too if I were you. But don't worry. The "words" will work for you. You will be more successful at everything you do. And you'll enjoy it far more, too! Or the book won't cost you a dime! I'll reveal the secrets of how to:

- Always get the best table in any restaurant in the world. (And you won't have to spend one cent in tips to get it!) (page 11)
- Often get first class or business class seats on an airplane, even though you have coach tickets. (page 13)
- Have employers clamoring to call you with job offers, even during tough economic times. (This powerful technique never before in print anywhere will boggle your mind and get you the job you really want!) (page 19)
- Attract all the money you need for any business venture. (page 25)
- Approach an attractive woman or man and immediately interest them in you. (page 24)
- Rent a Mercedes automobile for the price of a Ford anywhere. (page 35)
- Find a great gourmet cook to prepare low cost meals for you. (page 39)
- Slash the cost of lodging in first class hotels by 50% or more. (page 21)
- Get invited to speak before any group you choose and enhance your career. (page 43)
- Receive free expert consulting help for your business. (page 38)
- Buy beautiful jewelry, including gold rings and watches at below wholesale. (page 40)
- Earn over $100,000 in the most profitable business in the world, and start it for under $600. (page 42)
- Find world famous people to speak before your group, free. (page 59)
- Attract the world's best employees using can't miss ads. (page 63)
- Get capable people to work for you for free. (page 67)
- Get free advertising by becoming a celebrity first locally, then nationally. (page 56)
- Obtain the U.S. rights to market best selling products from around the world for as little as $250. (page 77)
- Reduce or eliminate legal fees in both your business and personal life. (page 62)
- Buy valuable antiques at huge discounts. (Page 85)
- Get valuable, financial interests in other people's companies without investing one red cent. (page 89)
- Earn from $100,000 to $250,000 a year and more as a consultant by making an offer almost no one can turn down. (page 93)

A special section of my latest successful print ads and mailings is included that reveals powerful strategies which can earn you $500,000 or more on your products!

Sworn Statements

"I was Ted Nicholas' bookkeeper for 7 years and helped prepare his tax returns. To the best of my knowledge, everything he has stated in this message is absolutely true and accurate."
Gail Waterman

"I've known Ted Nicholas for some time now. He is a charming man and highly successful writer and speaker. However, when he told me of his new book I was more than skeptical that these ideas would work this side of the Atlantic. He gave me three ideas to try out for myself.

1. Within 4 weeks I found the best personal assistant I've ever employed.

2. I got free business advice that has already been worth over £20,000 to my company.

3. I now ALWAYS get the very best service at every restaurant I visit.

Now the book is ready I can't wait to work my way through his other great ideas!"
Mike Chantry
Hilite Ltd.
London, England

Special Offer

A limited edition of this remarkable book is ready. You are now able to reserve a copy while supplies last at a special price if you order now. To avoid disappointment, call immediately (800) 730-7777. Fax to (813) 596-6900 or complete the coupon below.

Money Back Guarantee

After you receive the book and examine it for 60 days, if for any reason you are not completely happy, return it undamaged for a prompt and courteous refund.

☐ Yes. Please rush a copy of MAGIC WORDS THAT BRING YOU RICHES, by Ted Nicholas at $19.97 plus $4 shipping & handling. I understand that if for any reason I am not delighted with the book, I may return it undamaged for a prompt and courteous refund.

☐ Enclosed is my check
☐ Please charge my:
☐ Visa ☐ MC ☐ AmEx

Card Number _____ Expires _____
Signature _____
Name _____
Address _____
City/State/Zip _____
Daytime Phone (if we have a question on your order) _____

Nicholas Direct, Inc.
Dept. 00-0
P.O. Box 877
Indian Rocks Beach, FL 34635
© 1995 Nicholas Direct, Inc.

Ad used as basis for infomercial

real success stories that can be filmed and added to the infomercial to keep it fresh and current.

Just drop me a short note describing your experience and I'll discuss it with my producer for possible filming. If your segment is selected for the infomercial, you would really help spread the word. And the exposure may benefit you personally in your business.

Do I recommend infomercial producers?

I hesitate to recommend people in this field. And while there are a few capable and honest people, there are also many who, unfortunately, are not ethical. Plus, changes are going on all the time with people, companies, etc. Therefore, here is how I can best help you.

If you have a proposal in mind, send me a one-page fax describing it. I will either assist you myself or refer you to someone else.

So, do you still want to do an infomercial? I trust you are in better position to determine your own answer.

P.S. An excellent book on the background of infomercials or long form advertising that can be tough to find is entitled "Or Your Money Back" by Al Eikoff. Ask your bookstore if they can track down a copy for you. (I don't even recall the price of my old edition.)

Secrets of Profitable Yellow Page Advertising

I'm going to talk about a very important yet little understood media—yellow page advertising.

I love yellow page advertising! Reason? It is a marketer's dream. Unlike other media, it is the only form of advertising where most prospects are **ready to buy!**

Your business may be like many—totally dependent on yellow page advertising. Or the yellow pages may be a small part of your advertising budget.

Either way, *effective* yellow page advertising can *substantially increase your sales and profits*. And after reading and absorbing this issue, you will undoubtedly get far better results from your future yellow page advertising.

Yellow page advertising has long been a subject of great interest to me. Reason? In my observations, more dollars are invested badly in the yellow pages than in any other media. Possibly as much as *90%* of yellow page ad budgets are *wasted*. My reasons will become clear to you.

Look at the startling facts

In the US, according to research conducted by The Gallup Organization, 34% of the population consults the yellow pages before making a purchase!

Think of it! Approximately 1/3 of all buying decisions are made after being exposed to a yellow page ad!

How many references are made to yellow pages by US adult consumers each year? A staggering 19.4 billion references. And, of these references, 58% of the people who contacted an advertiser made a purchase. Now let's do some quick arithmetic. I don't know how much was spent. But if each buyer spent an average of $20, yellow pages account for at least **$250 billion dollars in sales!**

Amazingly, as powerful a medium as it is, the ads in my view are more poorly prepared in the yellow pages than in other established print media, including newspapers, magazines and card decks. Yellow page advertising uses largely a "me too" approach with advertisers blindly following each other. As the saying goes, it really is the blind following the blind.

What's wrong with most yellow page ads?

The short answer—almost everything!

Let's look at specifics.

1. More than *95% have no headline*! While so elementary, the vast majority miss the biggest sales opportunity of all—*starting with a benefit-driven headline*. Many studies show up to 80% of readers just read headlines. The headline can often be the best place in the ad for your unique selling proposition (U.S.P.).

2. *Size*. Most *ads are too small* to do a good job. This reduces both readership and response.

3. *Lack of benefits in the copy.* Any ad message is more effective when strong user benefits are used throughout the copy.

Most existing yellow page advertising stresses *features* or listings of products offered, not benefits. Features or listings do inform. But they miss persuading the prospect to buy. All *great advertising persuades.*

4. *No offer or close.* You must ask the prospect to take a specific action, to call you or otherwise close the sale. Yellow page ads usually do not make clear what action is required.

5. *No special incentives*—samples, bonus or free report or booklet—are used in most yellow page ads to motivate a prospect to call.

6. *No testimonials.* One of the most effective advertising strategies is the actual words from your satisfied customers, as this increases credibility. Seldom do you find testimonials when you review yellow page ads.

7. *No photos are used.* Photography can vastly improve the pulling power of yellow page ads, yet less than 1% include them.

8. *Ads look like ads.* Your ad message will get far more readership if they are filled with information, such as benefits, and look more like editorials, sometimes called "advertorials."

9. *Poor graphics.* If your yellow page advertising contains hard-to-read typefaces or poorly reproduced photos, you will miss many selling opportunities.

10. *Money back guarantees are seldom used.* One of the most effective strategies to increase sales and credibility is guarantees, yet they are almost non-existent in yellow pages.

11. *Ads are dull and boring.* The biggest sin in advertising is boring the readers. If you really want to see some deadly boring copy, take a hard look at your local yellow pages. Ugh!

How to make big money with yellow page advertising

You have *unlimited opportunities* when you approach yellow page advertising correctly. Plus, operating as a small company or even an individual proprietor, you can *outgun the big guys*. Even major corporations. Here is how.

The first secret is perhaps the hardest to practice. I must warn you—**You've got to be tough!**

You will be told over and over the techniques I'm about to reveal to you are *wrong*! Most yellow page publishers, competitors, professors, ad agencies, friends, relatives, your children—probably even your spouse—all will say you are off the wall! Dead wrong!

But I'm not here to argue with anyone. My goal is just to help you sell more products and services via yellow page ads. As with most of any successful life, you must go against conventional wisdom. To win big, here is what you must do.

1. *Always include a headline*. Your headline can be long. Up to 17 words. Tell your prospect what's in it for him/her. Start your ad with the most powerful benefit-driven headline you can create.

Always make a statement and answer this question in the mind of your prospect: "So what?" Most yellow page advertising headlines, over 97%, are simply the name of the company.

Do not use your logo or other "me" messages as a headline. Use "*you*" messages. For further details on creating headline see my book "Magic Words That Bring You Riches".

2. *Size of ad*. Invest in the *largest ad you can afford*. Your initial advertising investment may be more. But this is not the main consideration. Your response per dollar invested will be higher. Return on investment is what really counts in all advertising. Plus, remember—the more you tell, the more you sell.

The studies also show that if you get X response with a 2" ad, you don't get 2 times with a 4″ ad. You will get response in the order of 5 times. Or even 10 times in some cases! A quarter page ad can increase your response multiple by 20 times over an ad costing just ¼ as much.

A significant advantage of a large ad is that in the mind of the consumer it puts you on an equal footing with large local and even national companies. And remember, in marketing *perception is reality*.

If your yellow page ad supplier limits you to ¼ or ½ page, as do some directory publishers, take the largest ad size available.

3. *Fill your ad with benefits*. Benefits are what sell. Beginning with the headline and throughout the copy, show benefits of your product or service. If you have a creative block, here is a simple headline that you'll find is better than most other yellow page ads.

"Six Reasons Why You Should Choose (Your Company Name)"

4. *No specific offer or close*. The most effective action that your prospect can take after they read your ad is to call you.

Don't assume anything. Be specific with actions you'd like the prospect to take. Say things like, "For complete information or answers to questions without obligation of any kind, call toll free 1-800-000-0000."

5. *Use special incentives* in your ad to prompt a prospect to call. A free sample or gift can help increase the number of calls you get. What I often use is a free report or booklet with a powerful title that helps induce a call.

6. *Use testimonials liberally*. When your satisfied customers give you success stories or glowing praise, this can be one of the most effective yellow page sales tools. Include testimonials in your ads. Often they can make great headlines, too.

Tip: *After getting a signed release, use full name of person who gave the testimonial, which should be in quotation marks.*

7. *Use photographs.* Good photos are far more effective than line drawings. But make sure they are taken by a professional photographer who knows you are using them for a yellow page ad.

Tip: *Always caption the photo as to what it is or who it is if a person.*

8. *Give your ads an editorial look.* Journalists are usually trusted while advertising copywriters are rated just above taxi drivers as to credibility. You will get far more response when your ads have an "advertorial" look, filled with benefits and other useful information for the reader.

9. *Use effective graphics.*

- Do not use reverse type like this

   It's hard to read.

- Use Times Roman like this.

- Do not use a lot of "white space." Yellow page space is too expensive to waste.

- Make your ad copy heavy without looking crammed.

- Do not set the ad yourself or let the yellow page publisher do it. Instead, hire an experienced professional graphic artist.

10. *Use money back guarantees liberally.* You will increase sales, especially with services, to extraordinary levels, as much as 5 times—500%—and more! For example:

"Guaranteed satisfaction. If our automobile repair isn't completely satisfactory to you, our service costs you absolutely nothing."

11. *Make copy exciting*. Avoid boring the reader. Use plenty of short words that help create mental images or pictures in your copy. Here are a few examples:

Delaware man *drives lawyers insane*!

Next time you speak, get a *standing ovation*!

Incorporate in *7 minutes or less* on the telephone!

How to *see or be a lovebird* this weekend!

Wage your own *personal tax revolt*!

In the next three pages I'm going to show you some yellow page ads and some I've prepared for this chapter. Several "before" examples were selected at random from the Clearwater, Florida, yellow pages. Please note that most of the ads have *not* been run and are for *illustration purposes only*.

Profit opportunities from effective yellow page ads are probably the biggest untapped source of profits for entrepreneurs in today's business world.

Use the strategies in this book. You will be head and shoulders above your competition.

Before

This ad has been running in the Wall Street Journal *and other business media for over 10 years. A Yellow Page test APTR is also being tested. (Ads successful in other print media can often become profitable in the* Yellow Pages.*)*

After

Before

After

Note: Rewritten (after ads) are in the first development stage. Final ads would contain photographs and other graphic elements.

Before | After

Would You Sleep Better Tonight Knowing Your Roof is Guaranteed Not to Leak?

Everyone dreads the all too common experience of a leaking roof. It can really be a nightmare, especially if there is a long delay in getting it fixed.

Only one roofing company, Arry's Roofing Services (ARS), has built its business and reputation on this simple principle and unprecedented guarantee, which no one else dares to make.

"Your roof is guaranteed not to leak for a period of 3 years from repair or installation date, or upon request you will receive a prompt and courteous refund or credit of every cent it has cost you!"

Additional benefits you get from Arry's Roofing Services:

- Professional and courteous staff. You'll be impressed by the special uniforms, impeccably clean.
- Arry's personnel prides themselves on always leaving a clean and neat work area instead of the mess most roofers leave.
- Staff is drug tested at regular intervals.
- Personnel is fully covered by workman's compensation.
- Same day services on repairs.

All types of roofs, including shingle, tile, built-up and single ply flat roofs.

For a free estimate, without obligation, call 584-9565 or 938-9565

Before

5 Reasons to Choose The McGaughey Electricians

1. <u>All work fully guaranteed</u>. Each job is performed in a manner satisfactory to you, or you get a prompt and courteous refund or credit.
2. <u>Experienced uniformed electricians</u> working in your home or office are <u>fully insured and bonded</u>. Customers love our friendly, impeccably dressed personnel.
3. <u>24-hour repair service</u> guaranteed after installation or the repair is on us.
4. <u>Cleanup after job is done</u>. Unlike other electricians who leave a mess, your premises are always swept, vacuumed and left spic and span.
5. <u>Free estimates</u>, of course without obligation.

Call anytime 734-4408
McGaughey Electric Inc.
368 C Spaulding Road
Dunedin, FL 34698

After

Before

How to Get a High Paying Job In a Top Beauty Salon

Professional training is absolutely necessary today to get a good position in the glamorous beauty field.
Since 1966, graduates of our academy have been hired by the top salons. Look at these benefits and training:

- Cosmetology with the latest updates
- Nails Basic and Advanced
- Skincare with European techniques and equipment
- Make-up • Waxing • Color analysis
- Massage therapy with hydrotherapy

Hair, skin and nail products at discounted prices
Placement assistance
Financial aid if qualified
Day Evening Full/Part Time Classes

For complete information without obligation
Call 347-4247

Loraine's Academy Inc.
1012 58th Street, N.
St. Petersburg
Tyrone Gardens Center

After

Before

**Trial Attorney Wins Big Money Damages
For Victims of Serious Accidents or Malpractice**

Experienced attorney fights for your rights and gets money damages for you, or his services cost you nothing. But you must qualify.

If you've been injured in an accident we can help. Our experience covers auto, motorcycle, death claims, malpractice, construction, boating, nursing home, security violations and workmen's compensation.

You can set an evening or weekend appointment in our office, in your home, or in a hospital.

Over 16 years experience. We are also able to speak Spanish.

**Call now for a free consultation
461-4438**

After

How to Increase Wealth By Licensing Your Product Overseas!

I'm going to discuss a subject probably of great interest to my readers—marketing your successful product outside your own country.

A lot of money can be made if you do it right. Conversely, large sums of money can be, and are, lost if you make the common mistakes. Indeed, if you set up your own overseas operations, it is not uncommon to invest hundreds of thousands, even millions, of dollars. And then lose it all due to a badly conceived marketing plan.

Recently a big name in Australian direct marketing circles told me the story about how in England, within 8 months of trying to duplicate his Australian operation, he lost nearly $2,000,000!

There are several methods you can use to market abroad. These include joint ventures, working through agents, importers, franchises, manufacturers, retailers and distributors. Of course, you can also duplicate your operation. If you successfully operate in one country, such as the US, England, Germany, China or Japan, given enough time and money you can probably set up a similar operation in another country.

However, rather than cover all these methods, most of which take a heavy investment of time and money, I will focus on the fastest, easiest, most effective and lowest cost method I've found to expand outside your own country—**Licensing!**

Licensing enables you to enjoy profitable sales for your products without investment or risk. Often you don't even need to visit the overseas country!

In this ever-shrinking world, you are probably missing out on a lot of profit opportunities if you don't market overseas. Best of all, with the help of modern communications, including fax, Email and, of course, telephone, it's *easier to do business worldwide* than ever before!

I submit that there is no more profitable and satisfying income than that of licensing. Someone other than you invests their time and money promoting your product.

You receive income in return for granting rights to your previously developed product. No further work is necessary on your part!

A few of the benefits of licensing your products

I. *No financial investment required.*

Your licensee is normally responsible for all distribution expense, including ads, mailings, warehousing and inventory. (An exception, of course, would be if you set up a joint venture.)

II. *Diversification.*

You earn added income for a proven product in a new market. Plus, you often learn new marketing angles you can use back in your home country.

Does the idea of a never-ending income stream appeal to you? One of the joys of licensing when you are in several markets is the ability to earn royalty income 24 hours a day. It's an unsurpassed high to know that somebody somewhere is buying your product 24 hours a day! When the sun never sets on the sale of your products and services, you are a global marketer.

III. *You need to expend very little of your valuable time.*

You normally need to know nearly everything about a new market. However, there is no need for you to study every detail of what is involved. Instead of your having to learn about such things as local and federal rules and regulations, available media, mailing lists, and local competition, your licensee assumes this major responsibility. Plus, you gain your licensee's expertise, which can be invaluable!

IV. *Overcome language barriers.*

There is no need for translators or to learn foreign languages, which of course would be necessary in some markets. Most licensee candidates already speak English, the universal business language.

What to look for in a licensee

Ideally, your prospective licensee possesses these qualities:

1. *Trustworthy.* There is no way to build a long-term relationship unless you are working with someone you can completely trust. As with all positive relationships, you must seek out people who display the world's rarest human quality. Look for those who **keep their word.**

2. *Experience with your marketing method.* Whether you are a direct marketer of single products, sell via catalogues, wholesalers, retail stores, distributors, agents, franchisees, etc., it is crucially important your licensee has at least 3 years of experience using the same distribution system as the one you use.

3. *Experience with your type of product or service.* Your results will be far better if your licensee is now handling your type or category of product.

4. *Sufficiently capitalized.* You need a licensee who has sufficient resources to do the necessary advertising as well as be able to stock your product.

5. *Is the right size for your needs.* I suggest you seek someone who has a large enough operation to do the job without being overly large, bureaucratic and slow moving. The ideal company is small enough to be "hungry" and entrepreneurial while being able to act quickly to capitalize on available opportunities.

Where to find licensee candidates

A. Other licensors can provide leads and recommendations. Just ask.

B. Recommendations from international banks, accountants, consultants, importers and distributors.

C. Referrals from Chambers of Commerce, especially if you own a US business.

D. Recommendations in books and directories.

E. Existing licensees of other products similar to or close to your field.

F. Advertisements in places such as *The International Herald Tribune*, the US, European or Asian editions of *The Wall Street Journal,* or newspapers and magazines in the country of interest to you.

G. Mailing lists of companies who market similar products to yours within the countries you seek licensees. It's simple to get yourself on these lists by simply asking to be put on or buying a product.

While not absolutely necessary, it is usually helpful to visit and spend some time within the country where you want to establish licensees. Nothing will give you a better feel for the many nuances of the local situation regarding the marketing of your products than spending time there yourself.

Get references and check them out

As with all important business relationships, it's prudent to exercise caution prior to entering a licensing arrangement.

At minimum, ask for 3 business, one bank, and 3 personal references. Also be prepared to supply your own references if asked.

After getting references, call and/or fax each of them. Explain you are considering a licensing arrangement with your licensee prospect and they were given as a reference.

Ask, "Can you tell me in confidence if your business dealings were completely satisfactory?" If the answer is no, of course, ask why.

You'd be surprised how often you will discover unfavorable information. Of course, you can proceed or not, depending on how important you consider the data to your future licensing deal.

Generally, when you get a less than favorable reference from anyone your prospects have themselves given you, it's probably time to drop negotiations and find someone else to be your licensee.

How to structure the licensing arrangement

Once you have chosen your best available candidate for licensing your product(s), obviously you need to negotiate terms.

The key elements of a sound licensing agreement include:

How to Increase Wealth by Licensing Your Products Overseas! 257

1. *Who the parties are* to the agreement—individuals, partnerships, corporations, trusts.

2. *What products or services are being licensed.* A clear, specific description is necessary.

3. *Length.* A very workable length is one to two years initially, automatically renewable on an annual basis.

4. *Cancellation.* The agreement should be cancelable by either party if notice is given 30 days prior to end of annual term date.

5. *Royalty.* The royalty percentage must be agreed upon and included in the agreement. Royalty percentages can be any sum agreed upon by both parties.

However, I like to work business deals that are both comfortable and profitable to *both* parties. A long-term relationship is what you should seek. This can only arise when both parties are happy with the deal. For example, if the royalty rate is 25% or more, it is rare for the licensee to make money. So I don't get involved in such deals, even when offered.

Profitable royalty arrangements are usually 5% to 15% of the retail selling price. I presently am involved with a number of royalty arrangements at 10%. I like it and my licensees are thrilled with this profitable arrangement. Because they also have the right to use my sales copy, they in effect have **a license to print money!**

I, too, am happy to spread my work and ideas around the world while earning large sums in royalty income. Recently I've entered a new agreement which will further enhance the current profitable set-up. The result will be to generate licensee income in a total of 123 countries!

6. *Use your ad copy and marketing plan.* The ideal licensing arrangement is an extension of what has proven to profitably work in a country like the US, Canada, UK or Germany. If the marketing works in one large country, there is better than a 90% chance for it

to do as well, and often better, overseas. Of course, it's prudent to encourage your licensee to use proven advertising and marketing whenever possible.

7. *What marketing method are you licensing?* Whether you use direct mail or space ads, card decks, package inserts, Internet, or TV, your agreement should specifically describe exactly the media your licensee may use to promote which product.

8. *Exclusivity.* Your licensee will more than likely ask for exclusive rights to, for example, use direct mail and space ads to market your product in a given geographic area or country.

This can be a good idea suiting the interests of both parties. The only downside is when you've granted rights and an area is tied up with few or no sales being made. The way to handle this is with a *minimum sales clause*. If a mutually agreed upon sales level is not achieved, you would have the right to replace the licensee in that country.

When you explain that you obviously cannot tie up an area without any sales activity taking place, you will not have a problem as any reasonable person can easily see this.

The minimum sales figure can only be determined arbitrarily. It's just an educated guess. For example, to maintain exclusivity with direct print marketing for many of my books abroad, the minimum sales figure is 50,000 copies per year. That means sales of approximately $1,000,000 on a $20 book and royalties are $100,000 as a minimum.

If the sales figure drops below 50,000, the contract becomes non-exclusive. In such a case I could cancel the contract or appoint other non-exclusive licensees.

Of course, I'm not especially interested in appointing new licensees and would in all likelihood only do so if marketing activity had practically stopped. I clearly make my licensees aware of this.

Sample License Agreement

Ted Nicholas, author and copyright owner, will license to _____ exclusive certain marketing rights to the following product in the form indicated _____ to be sold via this marketing method and no other in _____(country).

Exceptions to these rights are:

This agreement will run until _____(date). After the first year, Ted Nicholas has the right to amend the agreement to a non-exclusive basis or terminate the agreement if the _____ (country) sales of _____ drops below _____ per month. Should he decide to do so, he will give _____ 30 days notice in writing.

Either party may cancel agreement within 30 days of the end of each license year by giving the other party 30 days notice in writing. Absent such notice, agreement will continue year to year.

_____ agrees to pay Ted Nicholas 10% of all revenue (less any refunds made) for all the sales within _____(country) by _____. Accounts are to be completed monthly and royalties paid within 14 days of the month end.

The list of names and addresses of the purchasers will be co-owned by _____ and Ted Nicholas and will be offered for rental to non-competitive mailers. The profits will be split 50/50 (i.e., revenue less direct costs).

_____ is responsible for all costs involved in manufacturing, marketing, distribution, and administration.

_____ is to supply Ted Nicholas with copies of any advertisements, direct mail and supplements to the manual prior to use. Ted Nicholas will have the right to amend or veto any changes incorporated by _____.

Ted Nicholas will allow _____ to use all previously used ad copy used to promote _____ plus any subsequent updates.

Ted Nicholas is to make other related products available for _____ to market in _____(country) at separately negotiated rates. Where _____ buys the finished product from Ted Nicholas, the royalty will not apply.

_____ is to provide Ted Nicholas with full marketing results on request.

_____ will supply product in case lots on a wholesale basis to a limited number of select marketers as designated by Ted Nicholas. Price will include manufacturing and shipping costs, plus a royalty for licensee of $ _____ per unit. _____ will require any such marketer to provide names and addresses of buyers. Orders will be pre-paid.

Any dispute between the parties to this Agreement which involves interpretations of the terms of this Agreement shall be submitted to arbitration under the rules of the American Arbitration Association, and the finding of the Arbitrator shall be binding on all parties. Any other dispute concerning fulfillment of this Agreement shall be litigated in a court of competent jurisdiction. Legal interpretation of this Agreement shall be governed by the laws of the State of Delaware.

Signed for _____ on ....
(signature) ....

Witnessed by:

Signed for Ted Nicholas, on   ....

Ted Nicholas   ....

Witnessed by: ....

Exceptions to exclusivity

If you had any non-exclusive dealers or sales arrangements of any kind with others prior to appointing a licensee, just identify who these parties are in the agreement. By doing so, you can continue with them if you wish. In such a case, you grant an exclusive license with the specific exceptions noted.

9. *Advance payment or not.* You could negotiate an advance payment against royalties in any licensee agreement. This can run from $1,000 to $25,000 or more.

Although licensee prospects often offer advance payment, I generally don't require it nor accept the money. Here's how I look at this issue.

While payments up front may seem advantageous, payments against royalties are just an advance anyway. An advance involves money paid in anticipation of future sales generated from the future marketing effort. I'd rather the licensee invest capital in marketing the product. In the long run it produces more sales.

I feel it's far better to agree with a licensee on a specific marketing budget, i.e. $10,000 to $25,000 or more is typical. The money is invested in the sales effort instead of in advance payments.

On the preceding page is an example of a standard marketing agreement I use. While I'm not giving you legal advice, as I'm not a lawyer, as a valued reader you are free to model your agreement on it if you and your advisors so choose. Of course, make whatever changes or modifications are appropriate for your particular operation.

Licensing gives you an extremely powerful wealth-building tool. The information in this chapter puts at your disposal the methods of expanding the marketing of your products to other markets worldwide. Without investment or risk. And fast.

Plus, you'll have fun increasing your profits from all around this exciting world!

How to Use Two-Step Marketing to Return a Profit of $29,450 for Every 1,000 Leads!

You undoubtedly will be motivated to test or improve the surest and perhaps the easiest way to make money today.

Two-step marketing!

This chapter takes a look at one of my previous newsletter reader's successfully using two-step marketing. While the example is several years old, it's just as valid today. Indeed, today's marketing by the reader looks almost identical. An actual example and live case history can be a great way for other subscribers to learn this process. This is especially so in a niche market!

James Bradshaw sells bodybuilding supplements. He has masterfully accomplished perhaps the biggest goals of direct mail—making a great deal of money!

Here are the actual figures which he freely shared with us. James Bradshaw is getting average sales of $31,200 per 1,000 leads. Costs are just $1,750.

Average lead cost is $1.75. The average order is $240!

What's more, returned merchandise is virtually nil.

I agree with Denny Hatch, publisher of *Who's Mailing What*, who called Bradshaw's recent accomplishments "textbook correct" direct marketing.

On the following pages is the actual case history, along with examples.

It begins with Bradshaw's letter to me.

Dear Ted:

I was reading your DMSL on one afternoon, prior to our weekly marketing meeting, and used your ideas to spawn the strategy for our new marketing campaign!

Anyway, here's the story! Our business is selling bodybuilding supplements. First problem...every marketer in the industry has access to the same products! So, how do we frame a marketing strategy to sell what everyone else is selling?

The first thing we did was totally subordinate the product...and sell the results of using the product! The final results which, of course, are...Money, Fame, Women, Vanity...all the emotional triggers.

The idea was simple. Buy 3 of our supplements, use them for 10 weeks, and the guy who makes the most noticeable improvement in his physique wins 50 grand and an awesome Corvette--in general, the "dream life." At least, the "dream life" for a bodybuilder! (As you're probably aware, the majority of bodybuilders are extremely vain and egotistical. They are also very lazy when it comes to real work.) That's why the greed and vanity angles were used so much!

One other very important point. almost all (95%) of bodybuilders will never compete. They are called "gym rats"! They're "wanna-bees." However, this is our market! Competitive bodybuilders don't use legal supplements--they go to Mexico and buy steroids. My point? Notice the headline on the lead generator...

Attention All Unknown Bodybuilders!

Hell, they're all unknown!! That's why the tremendously low lead cost!

In a nutshell, that's the story. Pretty simple--as long as you know your market! That might be something to delve into in one of your upcoming newsletters...

Know Your Market!

If you don't... no $$!!

Ted, thanks again for all your excellent advice--you've helped my commission checks go through the roof!

Sincerely,

James Bradshaw

James Bradshaw

Letter from James Bradshaw to Ted Nicholas

Attention... All *Unknown* Bodybuilders and Fitness Buffs... Fame. Cash. And A New 1995 Corvette... Can Be Yours!

$50,000 Endorsement Contract!

Even If You Don't Compete, You Can Become An "Overnight" Bodybuilding And Fitness Celebrity...And Receive...

- ☑ **A $50,000 Endorsement Contract With A Leading Supplement Company.**
- ☑ **A FREE Trip (Valued at $3,000) To The Arnold Classic, And Meet Arnold Himself!**
- ☑ **A New '95 Corvette!**
- ☑ **Appear As A Celebrity Guest At The Mr. Olympia Contest And Mingle Backstage With The World's Best Bodybuilders!**
- ☑ **Get Featured In Popular Bodybuilding Magazines!**
- ☑ **Travel FREE To Fitness And Bodybuilding Shows All Across America! And Much, Much More...**

Dear Friend,

Yes... it's absolutely amazing...but true! Even if you're an <u>unknown</u> bodybuilder or fitness buff...

You Can Make Big Money And Become Famous Practically Overnight!

That's right! A <u>nationwide</u> talent search sponsored by a leading supplement company is <u>not</u> looking for athletes who developed their physiques with massive amounts of drugs...then lie and say, "I just use 'XYZ' supplement."

Take Spiro Kandis, (the guy in the picture with the 'Vette and babes). Spiro is 5'10" tall and now weighs a rock-solid 193 pounds. He'll never be Mr. America, or for that matter, Mr. Anything. But he looks great. He's "athletically muscular." Decent size, and great "cuts"! He's got the kind of body women go crazy over!

But it wasn't that way ten weeks ago for Spiro. He looked OK, *but nothing like he looks now!* He gained an incredible 21 pounds of new muscular bodyweight using an amazing new training and supplement program distributed by a company called Physique Augmentation Systems (P.A.S.).

The marketing team behind P.A.S was so impressed by Spiro's amazing transformation using this new, revolutionary program, they offered him a very handsome endorsement package. Cash, a Corvette, and fame!

And P.A.S. Is Looking For More Spokespersons...

Why? Because P.A.S is different. They know as well as you do, many bodybuilders who endorse bodybuilding supplements get their development from drugs...<u>not</u> training and supplement programs! It's kind of misleading, isn t it?

That's why P.A.S is looking for spokespersons who <u>don't</u> use drugs, and <u>don't</u> have perfect genetics. They're looking for average folks to test their new, scientifically-designed muscle and strength-building program!

According to Eric Wagner, President of P.A.S his group is looking for <u>real</u> people to hire as spokespersons—people who can truthfully say their gains were a result of testing P.A.S products and nothing else.

P.A.S Representatives will select the next Spokesperson on January 31, 1995 and another on March 31, 1995 based on who makes the most improvements in muscle size and strength using the new P.A.S training and supplement program.

Yes, you too can be a spokesperson for P.A.S and receive a $50,000 endorsement contract, a new Corvette, become famous, and get to know the "behind the scenes" superstars who rule the bodybuilding and fitness industry.

It's The Most Exciting Opportunity Ever Offered To Any And All Unknown Bodybuilders And Fitness Buffs!

But to take advantage of this amazing opportunity, you must ACT NOW!!

Here's all you do. Just pick up the phone and call **1-800-297-9776 (Dept. #757)** and ask the operator to rush you more information on how you can become one of the next P.A.S spokespersons!

Please hurry. As you can imagine, P.A.S can only sign a limited number of spokespersons...why not <u>you</u>?! Call Right Now, TODAY!

Void in AZ, VT and where prohibited by law.

Lead Generating Ad

Even If You're An Unknown Bodybuilder Or Fitness Buff...

Fame, Cash, And A New 1995 Corvette Can Be Yours!!

$50,000 Endorsement Contract!

Dear Friend,

Yes, it's true!! This is not a misprint!

Just like me, you too can become a spokesperson for a top supplement company...

And receive a $50,000 endorsement contract... a new 1995 Corvette (valued at $41,000)... a FREE trip (valued at $3,000) to the Arnold Classic... appear as a celebrity guest at the Mr. Olympia contest... get featured in popular bodybuilding magazines... and travel FREE to fitness and bodybuilding shows all across America!!!

Hi, my name is Spiro Kandis. That's me in the picture above with the two gorgeous babes. As you can plainly see, I'd never be a threat to walk off with the Mr. Olympia crown, or even win the Mr. Colorado contest.

But what do I care? I've got a "fat" endorsement contract... a new Corvette... nationwide publicity... and more women chasing

(next page, please)

---

me than I can handle! (Well, almost!!!)

I'm the happiest guy in the world! And you can be too.

Please listen to my amazing story, and I'll tell you how you can be in the same "boat" I'm in. Believe me, if it can happen to an unknown guy like me, who just a short time ago looked like I did in the picture below...

It Can Happen To You Too!

Here's what I looked like on July 5, 1994...

After Almost 5 Years of Training!

Maybe, on a good day, after I finished a workout and was "pumped"... you might be able to tell I lifted weights. Maybe! More than likely, you'd guess I was a "smooth" gymnast or swimmer! I guess I'm what you'd call a "Hard Gainer."

A few years ago I decided to take steroids to do something about my lack of development. My drug of choice was testosterone cypionate. And guess what? I grew like crazy!!!... in all the wrong ways!

My face grew all puffy and swollen. (It looked twice its usual size.) I grew "zits" all over. I grew angry and violent. And... I grew myself right out of my girlfriend. She just couldn't handle my mood swings and my new, ugly look!

The whole thing sucked! I guess it wouldn't have been so bad if I'd put on just a little muscle, but I got nothing. I didn't even get puffy and bloated (except for my face). At least then, I would have looked big in clothes. And to top it all off, the guy

(next page, please)

Pages 1 & 2 of 8-page Sales Letter Follow-Up

I bought the "cyp" from got busted and they put him in jail!

That Was My First And Last Encounter With Steroids!!!

For the last couple of years I've just puttered around the gym hoping to discover some new breakthrough that would put a little muscle on me. Just enough muscle so someone, anyone, would accuse me of lifting weights!

Then on July 2, 1994, my "ship came in." I noticed a guy working out alongside me at "Better Bodies Fitness Center" in Arvada, CO. He was wearing a tank top that said P.A.S.--"The Best Natural Way To Get Big."

This guy wasn't exactly Dorian Yates... but he had some "guns." They looked about 18 inches and had awesome peaks. I asked him, "What's this P.A.S. stuff and does it work?" He said, "P.A.S. is the Physique Augmentation System, and it's probably the best new training, nutrition, and supplementation system around. You tell me if it works!"

Then he handed me two business cards, one was his--James Anderson, Marketing Director, Physique Augmentation Systems (P.A.S.), and the other--Anthony Almada, Research Director, Experimental and Applied Sciences.

He said to call Anthony and tell him James said to "comp" me the NEW Physique Augmentation System™ and explain everything to me.

Then he just walked off! What the heck! I didn't have anything to lose. At least this stuff was FREE. Even if it didn't work, I wouldn't be out any money. That's a lot more than I can say for the other "programs" I've tried.

So I called Anthony at his research facility in Pacific Grove, CA (it's 98 miles south of San Francisco) and told him James said to call and for God's sake...

Please Send Me The New Physique Augmentation System A.S.A.P.!!

Anthony said he understood the "urgency" of the matter... but before he sent me anything he wanted to make sure I knew precisely how to use the Physique Augmentation System. He said if I didn't follow his exact instructions... it would probably be about 90% less effective than if used correctly!

So I listened to him... for 25 minutes!! But you know what? I completely understood everything he said. Although Anthony is a highly educated sports medicine researcher and has a Master's degree in Nutritional and Exercise Biochemistry from the University of California at Berkeley... he explains things in a

(next page, please)

---

very simple, straight-forward way.

I mean this guy really knows his stuff! In fact, much of Anthony's immense knowledge came directly from Dr. George Brooks, who is recognized worldwide for his contributions to the nutrition and exercise world. (Learning about nutrition and exercise from Dr. Brooks is kind of like taking basketball lessons from Michael Jordan.)

Anyway, after digesting all the information from Anthony... I said to him again...

"For God's Sake, Please Send Me The New Physique Augmentation System A.S.A.P."

He said he would under one condition! That condition being...

Under No Circumstances Do I Give Anybody His Number And Ask Him To "Give Away" Another Free Seminar Over The Phone!

(Anthony has been paid up to $125 an hour to reveal his best kept secrets on how to build muscle and strength!) He said the only reason he even talked to me was because James referred me.

Hey, no problem--anything to get my hands on this awesome new System.

It arrived on July 5, 1994. I followed the Physique Augmentation System instructions to the letter and in just 65 days I put on 21 pounds of new muscular bodyweight! 21 pounds! And let me emphasize "muscular." Not only was I growing like a weed, my definition was getting razor sharp. I was much bigger and "ripped." I simply couldn't believe it. And neither could James the next time he saw me at Better Bodies.

"Hey, weren't you the guy who asked me about P.A.S. a month or so ago? The guy I told to call Anthony Almada?"

"Yep, that's me."

At that point, James didn't even know my name, but said "We gotta talk." He told me to come by his office the next morning because he wanted to show me off to the rest of the marketing staff!

The next morning I showed up with my "before" P.A.S. picture (the one on the second page of this letter)... and after a little coaxing from James, took off my shirt and showed everyone my new muscular body.

Well, let me tell you, everyone was completely "floored" by

(next page, please)

Pages 3 & 4 of Sales Letter

my miraculous improvement!

It was a pretty wild scene. I was standing in a fancy office with my shirt off, hitting poses for a bunch of marketing guys wearing 3-piece suits!

Then someone blurted out a comment that would change my life forever...

"Why Don't We Use This Guy As Our Spokesperson Instead Of A Pro Bodybuilder?"

"Hell, it's common knowledge practically all of those guys get huge on drugs, then lie about it, and say they got that way using some supplement. Spiro would add tons of credibility to our new campaign."

Two weeks later, I "inked" the sweetest deal of my life. A $50,000 endorsement contract... a new Corvette... a FREE trip to the Arnold Classic (valued at $3,000), where I'll get to meet Arnold himself... an appearance as a celebrity guest at the Mr. Olympia... write-ups in popular bodybuilding magazines... plus I get to travel FREE to fitness and bodybuilding shows all across America.

I can't wait to meet Arnold (maybe he'll turn me on to some of his Hollywood connections!). And... needless to say, I'm now "stylin'" in my new 'Vette. I don't know what it is... my new muscular body... the 'Vette... the money... or maybe just my newly-acquired self-confidence...

But Gorgeous Women Are Flocking To Me Like I'm Elvis!

Gorgeous women who just a few months ago wouldn't have given me the time of day... or anything else for that matter! Now I can barely keep my "date schedule" straight!

I'm so happy, I'm almost speechless. Everything I've always wanted, I've now got! Muscles. Cash. A "bad ride." Women. The world's my oyster!

And listen...

You Can Have It Too!

The company that distributes the Physique Augmentation System is looking for more spokespersons. Guys who are unknown and not competitive bodybuilders. Average guys like me who weren't gifted with great genetics and don't respond well to drugs!

And they can offer you the exact same incredible endorsement contract they gave me. The 50 grand, the 'Vette, the celebrity

(next page, please)

---

appearances... the entire package!!! (The women are up to you!)

I'll tell you more about this in a minute, but first, let me tell you a little more about the NEW Physique Augmentation System.

Basically, the "System" involves following the Physique Augmentation System Training and Nutrition Program and taking a very precise combination of three outrageously effective (but legal) compounds... V2G™... GKG™... and Phosphagen™.

Each of these compounds play a role in supporting a phenomenon called "cell volumizing." "Cell volumizing" is when water and nutrients are forced inside the muscle cell. When water and nutrients are forced inside the muscle cell they expand the muscle dramatically!! But the interesting part is...

This Can Cause The Muscle To Look Even More Defined And Muscular!

It doesn't make you look puffy and smooth, which happens when water is outside the muscle cell. V2G, GKG, and Phosphagen all work to support the uptake of water and nutrients by your muscle cells!

And, not only do your muscles look bigger and more defined when they are "volumized," but you're also more likely to build muscle size and strength faster! Recent scientific studies have shown that when a muscle cell is "volumized," it can speed-up protein production and slow protein breakdown.

What this means is... by following the Physique Augmentation System Training and Nutrition Program and taking these three supplements in just the right way, you can create great conditions for new muscle growth!

Also, by taking this new supplement stack, you can greatly increase your muscles' energy sources, which can lead to dramatic increases in strength and endurance!

The NEW Physique Augmentation System can have a super-powerful, dual-effect on muscle size, strength, and endurance.

Not only does each compound support "cell volumizing"... they do this through different mechanisms in the body. It's like this. V2G by itself will help you out. So will GKG and Phosphagen!

Any one of them, just by themselves, can work very well. But Anthony Almada believes when you combine them in just the right amounts, they work even better. You may get a multiple effect when all three are taken in the correct sequence and in just the right amounts! (This is vitally important!!!)

When you use this powerful supplement stack along with the

(next page, please)

Pages 5 & 6 of Sales Letter

Physique Augmentation System Training and Nutrition Program...

**Your Body Could Burst With Monstrous
New Gains In Muscle Size And Strength!**

The *NEW* Physique Augmentation System *is the absolute best natural way to get big and strong I've ever discovered!!*

Now for a little bad news. As you can imagine, P.A.S. can't sign-up every "budding" bodybuilder in the country. They're a good-sized company... but they're not Nike®!

They're looking for 7 more spokespersons and they'll give them the same deal I got!

How will P.A.S. decide which 7 guys to choose? Simple. By having a "before and after" spokesperson try-out. The try-out starts now!! The next spokesperson (I was the first) will be chosen on January 31, 1995, and another one will be chosen on March 31, 1995.

But, I need to clarify something. To get the endorsement contract, you don't have to necessarily look better than everyone else. P.A.S. is looking for the guys who make the most improvement. There is a big difference!

And listen, even if you don't get a contract... the absolute worst result of using the Physique Augmentation System will be...

**You'll Look Better Than You Ever Looked,
Or You'll Get Your Money Back--Guaranteed!**

And get this. Another 75 "runner-ups" will get their profile (name, address, phone number, age, and picture) listed in a new "who's who of Physique Models." This is like a catalog of male fitness models that will be sent out to talent agencies, movie directors, TV commercial people, etc. **There is a huge demand for male fitness models who are built somewhere between a GQ guy and a competitive bodybuilder!**

A huge demand! So even if you're not in the top 7, you still might make some $$$ off your new muscular body!!

So all in all, you've got absolutely nothing to lose and everything to gain. Fame, cash, a new muscular body, everything!!! There is no risk whatsoever when you use the NEW Physique Augmentation System.

And here's the best news yet. This new System will be "retailed" to the general public in the spring of 1995 for $5.16 a day (A 10-week cycle). But... for people who are trying out for the Spokesperson position this low price will be slashed even lower...

(next page, please)

To Only $3.41 A Day!!!
(A Huge Savings Of $122 Over 10 Weeks!)

Think about it--only $3.41 a day!!! That's about what you'd pay for a greasy breakfast at McDonalds®! This includes everything--a 10-week supply of supplements and the training and nutrition program--everything you need to build new muscle size and strength!

And... if for some strange and unexplainable reason you don't gain muscle size and strength using the Physique Augmentation System, you'll get all your money back--Guaranteed!!

You either get rich, famous, muscular, (or all three)... or you won't risk a skinny dime!

You simply can't lose!

But you must jump on it now!!!

At this time, a very limited supply of Physique Augmentation System Kits are available. This **NEW** System will not be available in stores until the spring of 1995. The only way to get it now is through this very exclusive Spokesperson Try-Out offer!

To take advantage of this "too good not to accept" offer, here's all you do. Quick--grab the phone and pound 1-800-297-9776 (Dept. #794), and have your credit card ready!

You've got to hurry though!

Believe me, with an offer like this... you can bet there's going to be some competition!!

But... you've got the same opportunity as everyone... to be rich, famous, and get a new muscular body!

Yours For The Ultimate Life!

Spiro Kandis

Spiro Kandis
P.A.S. Spokesperson

P.S. Yours Free! If you act now and are one of the first 75 people to take advantage of this amazing opportunity to become the next P.A.S. Spokesperson and become rich and famous... you'll get a Free one-hour body-building seminar on audio tape with Anthony Almada. Remember, Anthony has been paid up to $125 an hour for his expert advice! But you get it "Free" if you act immediately! So hurry, call now 1-800-297-9776 (Dept. #794) to order!!!

Spiro Kandis' extraordinary results using the Physique Augmentation System were witnessed and verified by independent sources. As individuals differ, so will results, but your satisfaction with the Physique Augmentation System is 100% guaranteed. Copyright© 1994 by Physique Augmentation Systems, Inc. All rights reserved.

Analysis—Key reasons why Bradshaw strategy worked

- *Market*—Media selection is correct for product. For example, Muscle Media 2000, Muscle Magazine International, Muscle Development, and Iron Man.

- *Emotional appeals* in copy correct for market.

    Headlines—

    ✓ **Attention . . . All Unknown Bodybuilders**
    Everyone wants to be discovered.

    ✓ **Fame**
    Nearly everyone wants to be famous.

    ✓ **Cash**
    Self interest is for money.

    ✓ **New Corvette**
    Highly appealing to audience.

    ✓ **Become Rich and Famous—Even If You Are Not a Competitive Bodybuilder**
    Applies to 99% of people.

- Photo—Suits purpose well. Male is not overly intimidating to average man and most men want to attract women.

- Copy—Powerful and appealing. Albeit sexist, has high believability with audience because it relates to many hidden inner desires

- Offer in letter—Full price is not stated. Instead, only $3.41 a day. Multiply $3.41 × 7 days × 10 weeks. This actually comes to $238.70.

- Follow-up Mailings—Bradshaw mails a total of 4 letters.

By studying the elements of this 2-step offer you can figure out how to adopt some of the same techniques to make your own offers more successful.

Is Money Important or Not?

Definition of Money: *A measure of value and medium of exchange. Money is usually issued by governments, backed only by government promises, such as the U.S. dollar, or fully backed by items of intrinsic value, such as gold, silver, diamonds, platinum, copper, nickel. The Swiss franc is the only currency in the world fully backed by gold. If a fully free society were ever organized, money issuance would logically be done by private firms, such as competing private mints.*

There is undoubtedly nothing in the world everyone spends more time discussing than money.

Countries go to war because of money. People marry and divorce because of money. Newspapers, financial newsletters, seminars, TV, radio and Wall Street pundits endlessly report on money and markets.

And we spend the biggest part of our waking hours working to earn it.

Yet, money may be the most misunderstood subject in the whole world.

A lot of ridiculous nonsense has been written about money by many people, including me.

Several things have caused me to think in more depth about money lately. I'd like to advise subscribers about my updated ideas and conclusions.

Should there be any question as to why this subject is being addressed in a marketing book, I submit this. The bottom-line purpose of all effective marketing is a surplus of cash (money) over expenses necessary to generate revenue. Therefore, I see money as a completely relevant topic.

I've stated that money is not everything, which is of course true. However, I want to put money in proper perspective. Money is *very important*. So much so, I've revised my views on what it takes to be a balanced and happy human being.

In my seminars, tapes and other materials, I often focus on the ideal being the right balance between three elements — health, career and personal relationships.

Human happiness rests on 4 elements—not 3

The happiest possible life ideally rests on a *balance between four elements*: *health, career, personal relationships* and *money*.

The *number one asset* we all have is *health*. No other value, including life itself, can exist without it.

Graphically here is how I view a balanced life:

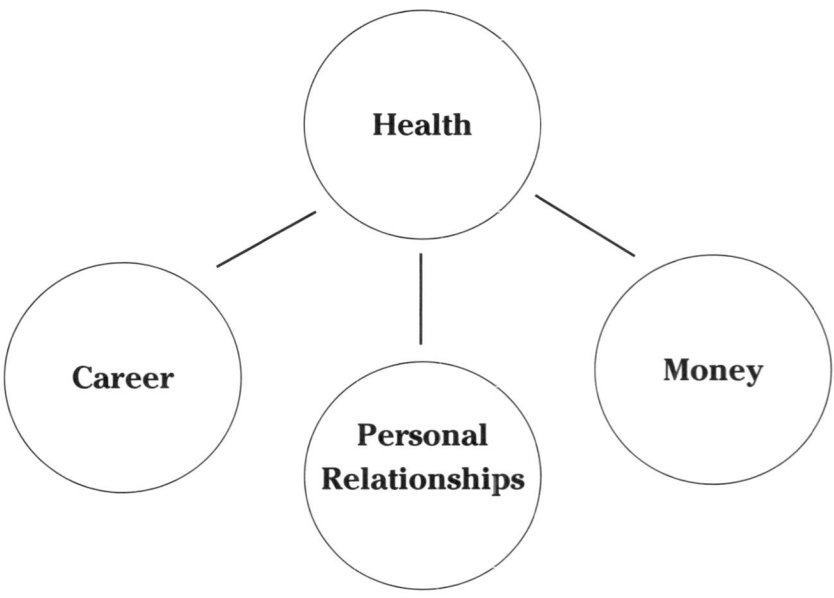

Why is money so important?

As previously mentioned in this book, here is what happens in America to a cross section of 100 men by age 65:

Out of every hundred men, age 25:

66 will live to age 65

5 will be working for a mere existence

4 will be in good circumstances

1 will be wealthy

56 will be dependent on their families, pensions, the community, or social security for the very bread and butter they eat.

As you can see, even in the U.S., the wealthiest country in the history of the world, only one person out of a hundred gets rich.

Money Statistics

When you take a look at the U.S. savings rate as compared with other countries, no wonder so many Americans are in trouble. The personal savings rate in the U.S. is now below 1% (in recent years there was even a negative savings rate!). Compare that to other parts of the world such as Sweden, Japan and Germany where savings rates average 11% and higher

My earliest fears about money

We're all profoundly influenced by childhood experiences. Here is how I first happened to think about money.

My father used to take me to buy Coward shoes. He always felt no matter how rich or poor you are, two things are an absolute must: comfortable shoes and a comfortable bed. Don't you think he was right?

During these trips we went to the Bowery section of New York where lots of people lived on the street.

Lying cold, unwashed with matted hair in abandoned store entrances, these poor souls made an indelible impression on me. One day I asked father, "These men must be pretty dumb to wind up like this, aren't they?"

His answer changed my life. He said, "That's not true. Most have at least average intelligence. Some even have a genius IQ. It's not the brainpower you have that counts. It's what you do with what you have."

I determined then and there I would never wind up homeless, living on the street. If I had to work three jobs simultaneously to make enough, I would do it. And one day I made myself a promise — I'd be wealthy.

After I started working, I saved at least 10% of my earnings, from the first paycheck on.

After starting in business at age 21, from profits I put aside 15% each week. I set the money aside in my pension profit sharing plan. I knew this money would be protected and saved for my future, even if my business failed.

My accountants told me I was a 'paper' millionaire at the age of 21 but I didn't feel rich! By the time I was 29, I had over one million dollars in cash saved up. The day my balance exceeded 7 figures was a big turning point in my life. Finally, I really felt that I was independently wealthy.

At the time, I didn't know a single person who actually had a million dollars in cash.

Sure, I'd met several who claimed to be "millionaires on paper" as I supposedly was. Being a "paper millionaire" is the premise that the liquidated value of assets as listed on paper less liabilities exceeds a million. The problem is many times assets can't be readily sold for the listed price "on paper."

Of course, a million in liquid cash safely in the bank can't be argued with. It's real. And in case you haven't as yet experienced this milestone, believe me, it's an unsurpassed thrill!

The predicament in which many find themselves

It's a proven fact that the average salaried person lives paycheck to paycheck. Savings are small or non-existent. The majority have less than $2,500 in cash. At retirement, most must rely on a meager income from social security.

Today, I have a few outstanding friends who are wealthy in real assets. However, among my friends and acquaintances are also some smart men and women about whom I'm concerned. A few examples:

- A 57-year-old lawyer and national political figure who was unincorporated, whose real estate and oil business failed. Being personally responsible, he was forced into bankruptcy and had to start over.
- A 54-year-old dentist who earns $125,000 a year who has not a penny in savings.
- A 69-year-old architect who lost his entire $700,000 savings trading commodities, a field in which even the experts usually wind up broke.
- A 60-year-old entrepreneur and business professor whose health club failed and is now unemployed.

While it's never too late to recover from financial setbacks, it can be more difficult the older you are. However, because you have the wisdom only experience can provide, this can definitely be a plus.

And, of course, there are well-known examples of people who made a fortune after age 65, such as Colonel Harlan Sanders with Kentucky Fried Chicken. He began with a social security check.

However, it's clear, the younger you begin putting together a financial nest egg the better. Time and compound interest can combine to keep the value of your savings growing.

In my view, the opportunities to become wealthy in the U.S. are unlimited for anyone who values wealth and does what is necessary. Anyone who does not have significant savings and wealth accumulated by age 55-65 to be able to live off the interest, has made a choice. Influencing that choice is an acceptance of one or more of the following sub-choices:

1. Choosing a job, business or profession in which the earnings are so minimal, savings are not possible.

2. Choosing to have no financial plan.

3. Choosing to rely on promises or income from the government, inheritance or a rich relative or friend.

4. Choosing to accept the common myth that money is unimportant.

5. Choosing to accept the common myth that there is some shortcut to wealth. Reality: There are not shortcuts. And I've looked too.

6. Choosing to accept the common myth that helping others and earning wealth are mutually exclusive. (I notice this view particularly among doctors and teachers.) Reality: The most giving people are often among the wealthiest. Plus, they have them means to be charitable if they decide, as some do, to take pleasure in giving some or even all of it away.

7. Choosing to accept the common myth that most business people are shady. Reality: While there are some crooks in business, 99% are honest. Otherwise, a long-term reputation upon which a business relies cannot be built.

8. Choosing to accept the common myth of live today for tomorrow you may die. Reality: Tomorrow you don't die.

9. Accepting this misquotation from the Bible, "Money is the root of all evil." Reality: What the Bible actually states is that "The love of money is the root of all evil," an entirely different concept.

10. Believing you don't really deserve to be rich. Reality: Every human being who is willing to take the appropriate actions deserves to be rich.

Instead of condemning money, I like best what the late novelist Ayn Rand said in her epic book, *Atlas Shrugged*, about money: "Money is the root of all good."

The world needs more rich people!

Who needs the rich the most? The poor! Why? Because capital accumulation is necessary for the creation of what the poor need most. Jobs!

Reality. Instead of feeling envy or resentment, poor people should do everything possible within their power to help the rich. For example, voting for reducing or eliminating tax on capital gains so that the wealthy have greater incentives to take risks.

A reduced tax on the highest levels of income would also benefit the poor far more than the rich. For a wealthy person, an increased tax reduces the capital available for investment purposes.

The late John Paul Getty, the wealthiest man in the world at the time, said: "The best thing I ever did for poor people is not to become one of them."

The best things about having enough money

Of course, you can go too far accumulating money and never feeling your wealth is quite enough no matter how rich you become.

How much is enough? Enough is the amount of money you need to live well without touching the principal and without the necessity of ever having to work again. Therefore, the best thing about money is:

1. *Personal freedom.* Money is the tool of independence. Complete. Total. Never having to do what you do not wish to do. Being able to live anywhere in the world is also a very liberating feeling.

2. *Charitable ability.* I enjoy being able to fund activities that interest me. While I oppose giving away money, as it usually does more harm than good, I'm especially interested in educational activ-

ities which help deserving people, such as the unsung heroes of the world—entrepreneurs. Also, the idea that accumulated wealth can continue to fund projects perhaps forever is exciting to me.

Americans tend to be the most charitable of any people on earth. In the U.S., the level of charitable contributions exceeds 100 billion dollars.

Entrepreneurs such as Astor, Carnegie, Ford, and Dupont and their heirs, through their charitable contributions, have done some remarkable things. Over 2500 libraries, untold university endowments, scientific and medical breakthroughs and housing assistance are but a few of the ways their bequests continue to carry forward the interests of these benefactors.

Here is a wonderful book on money

The most helpful book I've ever seen on the topic of money is entitled "Your Money or Your Life." Co-authors are Joseph R. Dominguez and Vicki Robin.

Here are some of the highlights from this book.

Do we value our lives more than money? Or the reverse? What we do for money dominates our waking hours and life is what we fit into what's left.

"Your Money or Your Life" is about how a person can gain control of their relationship with money and why that step is essential to achieving financial independence.

At the beginning of the book the following questions are asked:

1. Do you have enough money?

2. Are you spending enough time with your family and friends?

3. Do you come home from your job full of life and satisfaction?

4. Do you have time to participate in the things you feel are worthwhile?

5. If you were laid off from your job, would you see it as an opportunity?

6. Are you satisfied with the contribution you are making to the world?

There is a multi-step program in the book designed to transform the reader's relationship with money and lead to what the authors refer to as—**FI thinking—Financial Intelligence, Financial Integrity and Financial Independence**

1. *"How much have you earned in your life?"* The first part of this step is to determine how much you have actually earned in your lifetime, from the very first penny to the most recent paycheck. Because most of us have no idea how much we have earned in the past, we have no idea of how much we *could* earn.

Then determine your net worth by creating a personal balance sheet of assets and liabilities. Most people are worth more than they think. The whole purpose of this first step is to have a complete picture of your net worth, without shame or blame.

2. Step 2 establishes the actual costs in time and money that are required to maintain your job and compute your REAL hourly wage—*Money is something we choose to trade our life energy for.*

When we go to our jobs, we trade our life energy for money. We pay for money with our time. What this step does is put paid employment into real perspective and make clear how much you're actually getting paid.

3. After counting, tallying, adding and subtracting, Step 3 begins the process of evaluating the information you've collected. This obsessive counting is necessary to break the hold that money has over your life. Step 3 is the important process *of keeping a monthly tabulation of your money.*

4. To find fulfillment, you need to know what you're looking for. *To have a fulfilled life you must have a sense of purpose* and a dream of what a good life might be. All of us should take the time to envision what a truly fulfilled life for ourselves would be. Some interesting questions posed in the book are:

> What did you want to be when you grew up?
>
> What have you always wanted to do that you haven't done yet?
>
> What have you done in your life that you're really proud of?
>
> If you didn't work for a living, what would you do with your time?

Your spending should be evaluated by asking three questions:

> (1) Did I receive fulfillment, satisfaction and value in proportion to my life energy spent?
>
> (2) Is the expenditure of my life energy in alignment with my values?
>
> (3) How might this expenditure change if I didn't have to work for a living?

5. Step 5 is about getting your finances out in the open. Making a graph. Charting your expenses and seeing how they equal your life energy.

6. The authors point out that there isn't a word in the English language to define living at the peak of fulfillment, always having plenty, but not burdened with excess—a life of affluence *and* thrift.

Step 6 is about *minimizing spending*, something most Americans have trouble doing. "Your Money or Your Life" lists over 100 ways to save money. After all, frugality is cool again.

7. The next step is to value your life energy by maximizing your compensation for the hours you spend on your job. We must all do some work for basic survival. How much? Is there a daily requirement?

This step is about increasing your income by valuing the life energy you invest in your job and exchanging it for the highest pay consistent with your health and integrity. "Your Money or your Life" cites numerous case histories of people who have had to do a lot of soul searching, risk taking and challenging of belief systems to move forward.

"Your Money or Your Life" shows how you can realign your spending, earnings and consuming in order to lower monthly expense and invest the excess in safe, income producing vehicles. The goal is to reach the crossover point—Financial Independence—where monthly investment income crosses above monthly expenses. You will then be financially independent in the traditional sense of the word.

How Ted Nicholas Can Help You Further

- Free newsletter published on the web?
  THE SUCCESS MARGIN is published every two weeks as a free service for Ted Nicholas fans and readers.

  Plus, get on the mailing list for the latest valuable marketing information and breakthroughs. And important announcements. Stay connected. Don't lose touch. Contact website to subscribe: www.tednicholas.com

- Seminars
  For information contact website above

- Books and tapes by Ted Nicholas
  See website

- Consulting services include:
  Marketing/Consulting
  Copywriting

Share Your Success Story

Favorable publicity always helps an entrepreneur.

And to gain the attention and respect of your peers is always a good idea.

Plus, one of the biggest joys of success to experience is seeing your "story" in print.

You can also be an inspiration for other entrepreneurs who are truly in my book, the world's "Undiscovered Heroes."

If you prepare a short write-up of your success, 500 words or less, I'll do my best to help publicize you. Possibilities include my newsletter published on the Web, THE SUCCESS MARGIN, and future books.

If this book or other of my writings, tapes or seminars has helped you along your path, please describe exactly how.

The best way to send me your story is via the Internet at: www.tednicholas.com